Voice of Influence

Voice of Influence

How to get people to love to listen to you

Judy Apps

Illustrations by Helen Clare Brienza

Crown House Publishing Limited
www.crownhouse.co.uk
www.crownhousepublishing.com

First published by
Crown House Publishing Ltd
Crown Buildings, Bancyfelin, Carmarthen, Wales, SA33 5ND, UK
www.crownhouse.co.uk

and

Crown House Publishing Company LLC
6 Trowbridge Drive, Suite 5, Bethel, CT 06801-2858, USA
www.crownhousepublishing.com

British Library Cataloguing-in-Publication Data
A catalogue entry for this book is available from the British Library.

ISBN 978-184590288-9
LCCN 2009930316

Printed and bound in the UK by
The Cromwell Press Group, Trowbridge, Wiltshire

To John, Chris and Rosie

Contents

Acknowledgements

I would like to thank all who have contributed knowingly and unknowingly to the creation of this book, from my parents and family, teachers and other mentors to course participants, clients and people encountered on my way; and then there are all the people who have spoken to me through their writings. Thank you all.

I'm especially grateful to John Apps, Phil Hards and Peter Young for their valuable suggestions after reading the manuscript and to Crown House Publishing for their support.

Prologue

Gavin is in full flow. He excels at meetings. With his robust confident tones he easily takes charge as he numbers off the various problems besetting the company's publicity department in the current climate.

"There's the question of time frames," he explains. "By the time we've got everything settled, especially budgets, and launched our campaign, we're already into a different ball game: three months have gone and the market's already changed. That's exactly what Stephen said at the board last month."

June chips in with a couple of corrections: detail person June, always ready to put in her oar with a correction or a precise question or complaint: "I don't think that was *exactly* what the chair of the board said, was it Gavin? I think you'll find he mentioned two months, not three. It *is* the meeting *three* weeks ago you're talking about, isn't it?"

"Thank you June," says Bob easily, and goes on to the next point.

"It's all hopeless," grumbles Angela, "unless Finance stop being so tight-fisted, we're not going to get things off the ground at all. Someone's got to tell them they're standing in the way of this company's progress."

"Yes, that's right," agrees Raj. "Someone's got to tell them!"

Jim is sitting there observing them all. They have been around this scenario several times before. Something clearly needs to be done, and fairly fast, but all they do is talk. He's been thinking about the issue quite a lot himself, and has come to the conclusion that what's needed is a quicker way of getting to people; that is greater use of the internet and less time and money spent on long publicity campaigns that are out of date by the time they have come to fruition. The time has come for him to explain what he's been thinking but it's hard to get a word in edgeways at these meetings.

Everyone has so much to say and so little desire to listen to anyone else.

Still, it's what's needed, so he takes a grip of himself and waits for a gap to tell the others his idea. At last there's a brief pause and he takes his chance. "We need to start using the internet more," he blurts out rapidly. "Other companies have found it really successful. If we start spending money on Google Ads, we can monitor our results and use our budget in a really controlled way."

Angela glances at him, but June interrupts: "Don't talk to me about budgets. We've been waiting since April for a final confirmation of last year's figures and we need to speak to Peter about the reasons for the delay. I emailed him about it on the 5th, but he replied on the 7th that more time was needed. If we could just pin Peter down, we would be able to sort it ..."

"Right, if I can continue," announces Gavin. "So, to sum up, the main problems as I see it are ..."

Jim slumps back in his chair thinking to himself, "No one listens to me. I sometimes wonder why I bother to turn up at all."

The meeting proceeds on its erratic course.

Ten minutes later, Angela puts both hands out on the table. *"This"*, she announces in firm tones, arms out straight, "requires a radical—a *radical*—rethink. And what is needed", she continues confidently, "is something really different." She looks around.

"So I've been thinking." Everyone turns towards her expectantly.

She waits for their attention. "We need to work *quickly*, be more *responsive* to the market."

She pauses for effect, and then pronounces enthusiastically, "What we need is *Google Ads!*"

"*Google Ads*! You're right!" exclaims Gavin. "That's it! We need to use the internet more."

"Well, at last we have a really sound suggestion," approves June. "Great idea, eh, Jim?"

Jim bites his lip.

"This one will work," agrees Raj. "Good one, Angela."

"So we're all decided then," declares Gavin. "Look into more internet publicity, low budget, responsive, highly effective. Thanks Angela, I really think you've hit the jackpot there!"

* * *

I walk through the imposing portals of Sotheby's, the great auction house of London. I am carrying a violin which used to be my grandfather's. Its case is heavy and wooden, shaped like a coffin with the handle on the lid. The scuffing suggests much use; it has been played in military academies, in smoke-filled rooms, in the cinema for silent films. I want to know its value. But this building is intimidating and its processes unclear. I approach the reception with its high desk almost taller than I am. An official turns his eyes towards me without interest and gazes impassively.

I clear my throat. "Hmm, excuse me, I'd like …" My voice comes out pinched and high. "Er, that is, I'd like …"

And then I bring to mind for a moment my journey from timid young woman to someone who knows what she is about. I find my voice. It suddenly breaks out, deep and loud, and resonates around the grand hall: "I'd like to have a valuation on this violin, please."

The official is suddenly all attention and respect: "Certainly, madam! If you'd kindly follow me, I'll find one of our experts to attend to you! Er … have you come far?" And we enter into the heart of the building side by side.

Preface

There is no index of character so sure as the voice.

Benjamin Disraeli

So, what would you like to be able to do with your voice?

Would you like to sound stronger, be able to speak louder?

Would you like to sound more convincing, with more gravitas?

Do you just wish that people would listen to you?

Would you like to be able to express yourself with more light and shade, to engage people more and sound more interesting?

Would you like to know how to inspire people with your passion, influence them with your voice?

Do you want to use your voice to show empathy so that people realise you care?

Do you wish people would stop finding your voice an impediment to appreciating the real you?

You'll find the answers to these questions and much more in this book.

The book arises from observing and dealing with the problems and questions of voice clients in ten years and more of coaching. Over the years, I built up expertise in diagnosing what was wrong with the way people spoke and was on the whole successful in helping them to speak more effectively. But telling them what was wrong and helping them to know what to do about it did not work *every* time. As I worked with people, I became aware that when I taught the techniques of what various parts of the body should be doing to improve speaking skills, some people became *more* self-conscious and awkward, not *less*, and therefore did not improve as much as they should have.

In the late 1990s I immersed myself in the psychological practice of neurolinguistic programming (NLP) and realised how much there is to learn by observing closely people who are successful in any field (what NLP calls "modelling"). NLP takes a holistic approach to learning from successful people, discounting nothing at the outset, and employs a quality of awareness in observing the models that goes far beyond noticing the obvious presenting characteristics.

NLP emerged originally from modelling the practice of successful psychotherapists. The first models—the psychotherapist Fritz Perls, the family therapist Virginia Satir and the hypnotherapist Milton H. Erickson—were observed, imitated and questioned in great detail over a period of time, and from these studies certain patterns emerged which other people could replicate. Thus people could learn, through modelling, how to achieve similar results.

When a top practitioner in any field is modelled, in NLP terms, what emerges very often is that their success is based as much (and usually more) on their internal world—beliefs, values, attitudes and so on—as on their technical skills. Over the years of observing and listening to great speakers, I began to realise that technical vocal skill was not the starting point for their success, but rather the *result* of something far more important inside the speaker: their beliefs, values and attitudes, and purpose in speaking. This inner world created the voice, not vice versa. Based on this observation, I decided that in order to find out how to speak more effectively I would need to pay close attention to these inner factors too.

After my modelling discoveries, I found in teaching voice that people learned *much quicker* and also *more enjoyably* when we included such inner factors as state of mind, beliefs and so on. Far from being a "flaky" addition to proper teaching, it was the principal means by which students found their voice *and* saved months of physical practice of breathing, voicing and articulation.

So this is a how-to book, but unusual in that it goes beyond the usual remit of such books and investigates the inner connections of the speaker with the outer successful voice. This might seem frustrating at first as the externals of technique are more obvious for your conscious mind to grasp, but stay with it and you will find that it is a highly effective and rapid way to learn. Physical practice has its place as well, but much physical ability emerges quite naturally and instantly as a result of approaching things in this different way.

Be your note
I'll show you how it is enough.

Rumi

Part One

Get To Know Your Voice

Chapter One

Introduction

Your amazing voice

Your voice is an extraordinary tool of enormous potential benefit to you and others around you. Great leaders through history have used the voice to inspire and influence. From the days of Greek orators in the market place to current politicians and leaders at public events, the spoken word has always had the ability to influence an audience in ways that the written word cannot. The vibrations of the voice act on human beings in powerful ways. If you want to have influence you need to be able to speak with passion and determination: you need to know how to use your voice to best effect.

The sounds you make have a story to tell. As soon as you open your mouth your voice says much about you, not only about your state of mind in the here and now, but also about where you come from and how you have met life's challenges up till now. Your voice is very much tied up with *who* you are. If you want to develop your voice, you are embarking not only on a journey into different ways of speaking, but also an exploration of who you are at your authentic core and how you interact with the world.

Purpose of this book

Through reading this book, you will discover three powerful secrets:

- How to develop your voice so that you have more options in communicating with other people and the ability to adapt to different situations and exert influence.

- How to express different aspects of yourself, so that your ideas, thoughts and emotions on the inside are expressed authentically on the outside.
- And how to be more discerning in your listening, so that underneath the words and accent you hear more accurately what another person's voice is really saying and not saying. You'll acquire the ability to "hear inside" other people, just as some have the ability to "see inside" others. Learning to distinguish the nuances of voice, you will be able to hear the fuller message behind a person's words and discover much about their psychology, history and truthfulness. This is an effective tool for understanding others and a great defence against being manipulated.

Using both physical and psychological processes to develop your voice you will:

- Learn various physical techniques and then practise them to build your vocal fitness.
- Discover how to connect body and mind in your voice and get more in touch with yourself. Most vocal problems arise because your voice has been cut off in some way from your body and emotional life, so "finding your voice" becomes a process of reconnecting with yourself.

How to use this book

> Everyone should have a voice coach.
>
> Richard Bandler

This book tells the story of your voice, and you may enjoy a first reading without pausing too much for the exercises. There is plenty that you can learn through doing just that. Then go through again, trying the exercises and experimenting with some of the ideas to get your learning "in the muscle", that is, more instinctive and readily available to you.

The layout of the book mirrors a concept developed by the NLP developer and author, Robert Dilts, called the Neurological Levels. The concept proposes that different levels of learning demand successively deeper commitments of neurological "circuitry". There are six levels, which broadly work from outside a person to a more and more intimate connection to a person's core. The first level of learning is on the outside, getting the environment right for learning; the second level deals with *what* you do, your behaviour; the third with *how* you do it, your cognitive abilities; the fourth with *why*, what values and beliefs lend it importance; the fifth with how the learning expresses your identity; and the last with how it connects with your mission and sense of underlying purpose.

Each part of this book deals broadly with one level. So Part 1 starts with information *about* the voice, how it works, the story it has to tell and why people sound different from each other.

In Part 2 you learn *what* to do to speak effectively. This gives you the basics of how to produce your voice well, with valuable information on breathing, relaxation, voice resonance and articulation.

Part 3 shows you *how* to deal with particular voice issues. If, for example, people don't listen to you, or you lack confidence, or you don't seem to influence people in the way you would like, this self-help section gives you practical solutions to specific communication issues.

Part 4 gets to the heart of the matter to uncover the magic of the voice: *why* it is that some speakers influence us powerfully while others with good voices don't. Here you will find secrets from top influential speakers that are not often shared.

Part 5 brings the strands together to examine how your voice can express *who* you are. In expressing the real you, you find your true voice and through this the channel to influence others powerfully. This allows you to express the last level: your sense of mission and purpose.

In conclusion, the Appendix offers some advice for caring for your voice and suggests remedies for particular vocal problems such as hoarseness, tiredness and so on.

* * *

A book cannot entirely replace a voice coach for working on your voice, but it can be a helpful guide. There is much you can do alone and many discoveries to be made by trying out the exercises in this book with a playful and curious frame of mind. There's no set way to do the exercises—it's about experimenting, experiencing and getting feedback.

Hopefully, the book will also inspire you to find a live coach or a voice coaching course to discover more about the many ways in which you can be more confident, inspiring and influential as a speaker. My website http://www.voiceofinfluence.co.uk would be a good start!

But for now, sit back and enjoy the story of voice.

Chapter Two

Voices, voices

A successful public speaker such as Obama knows exactly
how to intonate his voice to excite or calm the crowd.
Speaking in just the right tone at the right time and pausing at
the correct moments in just the right way, can really rally the
audience.

Logan S. Freeth

No one sounds more like everyone's ex than Hillary when she
has that "you're stepping on my foot" tone.

Journalist Timothy Perry describing Hillary Clinton at
the July 2004 Democratic Convention

She sounded like the Book of Revelations read out over a
railway station public address system by a headmistress of a
certain age wearing calico knickers.

Clive James on Margaret Thatcher

Bush seems to have two separate voices, the "charming
Texas frat boy" voice he uses in informal discussions and the
"clipped, rapid, sound bite" voice he uses when conducting
official business.

Renee Grant-Williams, voice coach from
Nashville, Tennessee

She's been voice-trained to speak to me as though my dog just
died.

Keith Waterhouse on Margaret Thatcher

It sounds as if she were consuming a plate of spaghetti with a
fork and spoon.

Anonymous critic describing Janet Street-Porter's voice

His voice, with plummy stutter, is orotund.

Journalist Michael Wolff on Boris Johnson,
Lord Mayor of London

> In every matchup of the last forty years, the candidate who
> had the most resonant, deeper and more expressive voice won
> ... This clearly favors Sen. Obama, whose voice is unparalleled
> in modern politics.
>
> Blogger Patrick the Rogue, before Obama won
the 2008 Presidential Election

Voices, voices ... everywhere voices: radio, TV, DVD, internet, people in shops and pubs, at work, at play; each person a different voice. What can we make of all the different sounds that come from human beings?

Some people talk seemingly just for themselves and their voice never reaches the listener. Some speak right out, almost overwhelming you with the sound of their voice and seemingly only interested in communication as a one-way street. Others speak so carefully and correctly they sound as if they are reading a script. Some seem to have difficulty in dragging their voice out from their inner depths. We talk about warm voices, strong voices, cold voices, weak voices, rich, weighty, bright voices. There are certainly many different ways to communicate!

The voice that people hear is just sounds, but what information those sounds hold! Your voice is a blueprint of you. Your accent tells where you come from and where you have spent periods of your life. And your tone of voice reveals your attitude, your confidence, how comfortable you are in your own skin and other emotions and feelings.

Your voice also tells the story of your past emotional life, revealing in its freedoms and tensions the way you have met life's ups and downs. It shows your truth and your falsehood, your life energy and intention.

Voice language/body language

Human beings have five senses with which to take in information and communicate, and three of these in particular, sight, sound and touch, come into play when we communicate with each other.

The visual element of communication—body language—has become a popular topic of our times and many books have been written about these non-verbal clues to communication: posture, hand gestures, facial expressions and so on. We have all become quite good at noticing the tics and tags of our leaders: little signs of discomfort in interviews, the subtle pointers to lack of ease when politicians express opinions, the micro-movements that betray lack of sincerity.

Malcolm Gladwell, in his entertaining book, *Blink*, tells how the psychologist Paul Ekman succeeds in catching on tape the smallest of visual clues that a person is lying. When the spy Kim Philby is asked if he has committed treason, Ekman describes the fleeting millisecond of facial expression that crosses Philby's face, "like the cat who ate the canary", before he resumes his serious demeanour. We catch a minute glimpse of the spy's pleasure at duping his interviewer.[1]

How people speak—the sound they make—has been investigated much less by researchers into communication. And most of us, apart from perhaps noting a regional or class accent, distinguish very little: high voice, deep voice, squeaky voice, rich voice, we tend to leave it at that. In the Philby episode, nothing is detected from his voice. Philby answers confidently, "in the plummy tones of the English upper class". Does his voice in fact give nothing away? How much can the sounds someone makes tell us about them? Is sound as accurate an indicator of someone's inner life as sight?

Well, yes it is. There is a whole world of information to be discovered through the sounds that people make. And if we want to influence others, we need to know what that information is, so that we can use our voices in ways that work for us, and not against us.

The art of listening to the nuances of voice goes back a long way. The sixth century Chinese Buddhist teacher T'ien-T'ai writes that the voice is a subtle mirror of our inner wellbeing, revealing our mental state and our physical health to someone who knows how to read the signs. "How can you tell a fine physician?" he asks. "The inferior physician feels the pulse, the ordinary physician observes the patient's colour, and the superior physician listens to the patient's voice."[2]

The psychotherapist Fritz Perls also talks about listening to the actual sound of the voice beyond the words: "A good therapist", he says, "doesn't listen to the content of the bullshit the patient produces, but to the sound, to the music, to the hesitations."[3]

Most of us would not claim to have an auditory sensibility as acute as his. Yet some people do acquire listening skills to an extraordinary degree. I was once discussing voice in a group that included a television producer. She told the group that she felt her voice gave her away too much, and she said it in a voice that had a persistent harsh metallic twang. Members of the group glanced at each other. It was a curious statement to make, as her voice just didn't seem to vary at all whatever she said. But she explained that if she telephoned her daughter, the young woman knew instantly if her mother was happy or troubled.

I later discovered that it was a skill she had learned very young. As the daughter was growing up they had lived through unstable times as a single parent family, with many house moves and different confusing relationships. The child had felt fearfully responsible for their joint safety and happiness. As a consequence she had at a young age acquired an acute auditory sensibility to her mother's voice to be able to know her state of mind and judge how things stood. She was aware of its every nuance even though its timbre varied so little. Necessity had allowed her to develop a listening skill that most of us never develop.

Our senses can certainly be tuned to greater awareness. A few people have a highly developed sense of taste and smell and are able to tell you exactly where a wine comes from. They sniff the glass, look at the colour, take a sip and roll the wine around in the mouth for a moment, then announce, "Mmm … it's definitely Montepulciano. I think it comes from one of those fields on the left as you take the road down from Pienza …" The rest of us can only gape in amazement and admiration.

There are people who can do something similar with an accent—"Mmm … Cambridge … south Cambridge … the Shelfords, I should think"—though this may be an increasingly rare skill. We now all move around so much and encounter such a variety of accents that our own accents tend to be less distinctive than once they were.

Accents

Your accent is one aspect of the sound you make. We might call the accent the surface structure of the voice. Across the world people speak in different languages, and across the English speaking world they speak in different accents. Accents are an integral part of the glorious variety of human sound. In many countries, people are proud of their regional accent. In Italy, for example, people love to speak in their local accent if there is anyone around to recognise it. People can be fiercely loyal to where they come from and show this loyalty through love for their local way of speaking.

In England, the reverse is often true. Accent is still so tied up with class that it can feel like a handicap to people who originate from certain regions. We see the funny side when a comedian like Bill Bailey does an imitation of James Bond in a West Country accent. Mix up a film track of a well-known politician speaking in "received pronunciation" with a voice with a strong regional accent, and comedy is not far away. Received pronunciation: the very term sums up a closed way of thinking. Many people seek to change their accents in order to advance their prospects and career. Others perpetrate a kind of vocal racism in their attitude to those with different accents.

But accent is for a different book. Accent alone does not reveal the personality in the way that the vibration of the voice does. Beneath the surface structure of accent we all express common energies, such as love and anger, openness and inhibition, wanting, generosity and empathy. The deep structure of voice is the vibration through head and body that gives life to the sound; that is, not accent, but the inner life of timbre, pitch, tone, speed and rhythm. Those are the sounds we are going to learn to identify and understand better.

When you are in tune with what you want to say, your voice will naturally express your emotions and intentions in its sound. Projecting the full richness of expression in the vibration of your sounds, you become influential and others respond. But when you guard your communication, your voice fails to respond freely and you become cut off from true expression. The voice becomes a dull instrument or a mask. As you learn to become a voice

11

"connoisseur" and can discern the nuances of the vibrations in the voice as accurately as the wine buff can appraise a wine, you have a wealth of information about the other person. You will also hear when that information is missing because the voice is inhibited.

What do you *sound like?*

Attempting to develop your voice by concentrating on the actual sound you make is a thankless task because you never really know what sound you are making and no recording equipment ever quite captures the entirety of your voice.

Have you sometimes heard your voice in a recording and been disappointed? Very often it sounds higher and thinner than you are expecting. This can certainly be partly due to shortcomings in the recording apparatus, but it is partly that we cannot recognise what we sound like as we never hear ourselves as others hear us. The sound we hear ourselves when we speak is a sound felt and heard internally through our own bone vibrations more than heard through the air from the outside. This internally heard sound can be deceptively resonant and full compared to the sound others hear. We are also influenced by how we want to sound, so our ability to hear ourselves is remarkably subjective.

To get a rough idea of what you really sound like, experiment with the following.

Listen to yourself

With one hand, bend one ear gently forward and cup the hand behind the ear. Hold the other hand in front of your face a few centimetres away from your mouth, gently rounded with the fingers pointing towards and almost touching the other cupped hand. Then speak into the rounded hand in front of your face. Experiment with moving the hand in front of you a little closer or further away. You will hear a sound that approximates to the sound others hear when you speak.

It's just sound, isn't it?

We often refuse to accept an idea merely because the tone of
voice in which it has been expressed is unsympathetic to us.

Friedrich Nietzsche

What happens when someone speaks to you? They make sounds,
and you make meaning from those sounds. The meaning you
make comes from two elements: the sense of the word in terms of
language and the actual sound of the word. As most people tend
to value the rational brain more than emotional responses, you
might assume that you lend more importance to the sense of the
language; after all, that's what the word is really about, isn't it? But
in actual fact, you are probably influenced more by the sound than
by the sense, as will become clear.

Historically, language started with sound. Animals make sounds:
mating sounds, alarm sounds and contented sounds. The sound
of human language is often closely connected to the sense.
Onomatopoeic words such as "murmur", "click", "pop" and
"whirr" imitate the sounds they describe.

There are other examples of phonaesthesia which connect to meaning in looser ways. For example, words such as "beaten", "battered", "bruised" and "bashed", associated with hitting, begin with
"b", a satisfyingly plosive consonant. Other sounds are expressive
because of the way we use our physiology to produce them. For
example, the sound /sn/ is created most easily by wrinkling the
nose, a gesture associated with disgust or disapproval. When you
investigate words that begin with /sn/, many contain within
the sound that negative connotation: "snarl", "snide", "snatch",
"snitch", "sneak", "sneer", "snivel", "snob". The consonants help
the transmission of meaning. The long soft sound /m/, on the
other hand, which encourages the mouth to smile, is associated
in many languages with gentle meaning: "mother", "maternal",
"mmm" (sound of appreciation) and so on. It is obvious in such
words that sound connects directly with what we want to express.

This connection between sound and sense is in fact true with every
word. The expression we give to the word—the actual sound we
make—plays a part in determining the meaning. Each word can

be spoken in infinitely different ways. If the dictionary definition of the word were all that counted we would listen to each other's words for meaning only. But we all know that the same words can be convincing when spoken by one voice and weak or hollow when spoken by another. It's the actual sound that gives us the biggest clue to what the speaker intends.

Try shouting "I love you" in a loud harsh voice. What does such an utterance mean? Maybe something like, "Don't you dare leave me. You're mine. You'll be sorry if you abandon me." Now say "I love you" in a whining, needy voice. This time the meaning might be closer to, "Don't leave me! I need you. I'm lost without you." Now think of someone you truly love, conjure a picture of them smiling at you, and say the words again, "I love you". Different again, isn't it?

The sound is created by an inner energy and movement of your breath and parts of your body. This is vitally important when you start to work on your voice, because a highly effective way of developing a more expressive voice is through working on this inner energy and movement, rather than concentrating on the actual techniques of the sound you make. Your expression is created by the *motion* of thoughts and feelings from the inside to the outside world. The word *emotion* shares the same derivation.

Vibrations

> Music is feeling, then, not sound.
>
> Wallace Stevens

Looking at the three senses, sight, sound and touch, sound and touch have something in common that sight lacks. When you look at someone, your eyes do not produce a *physical* connection between you—even when you feel electricity across a crowded room! But when you hear the words of another person, the vibrations of their voice—the actual waves of sound—enter your body as inner touch. When you speak yourself, you also produce your own body vibrations. You are "moved" or "touched" by sound in a literal way.

As sound has this ability to connect intimately through touch, the language of sound is often used to describe our relationships with other people. You find that you are *on the same wavelength*. You are *in tune* with each other. They say things that *resonate* with you. You want your relationships to be *harmonious*.

Hearing and feeling refer to two different senses: sound and touch. But in some languages, the same word is used for both without distinction (Italian *sentire* for example). The remarkable deaf percussionist Evelyn Glennie makes brilliant use of this connection between hearing and feeling. She *feels* sounds in her body with such a degree of sensitivity that she can perform successfully as a professional musician. Most of us understand the connection between sound and feeling when we hear/feel the low vibrations of a large truck passing by, but unlike most of us she has acquired sufficient sensitivity of touch to feel tones through a large pitch range.

The kinaesthetic effect of sound may be why we are all particularly affected by people's voices. Another person might impact on you visually and arouse a feeling in you by what they wear or how they present themselves. But when you meet someone who opens their mouth and screeches—or speaks with a whining, moaning, nasal, metallic or harsh voice—that vibration disturbs your being in a literal way and creates an instant change in your state. You can shut your eyes to stop seeing but you cannot so easily shut your ears. There are times when some of us wish we had ear-lids!

Still, the converse is also true: if someone can have a strong negative effect by how they sound, they can also affect you positively with a sound that resonates harmoniously with you or stirs you with its passion.

The greatest speakers through history have found a way to use words not just to communicate knowledge and information, but to connect with their listeners and to move them. They have achieved this by creating sounds that are harmonious and reach out to their audience. Their power is expressed through a voice that is in contact with who they are, so that their inner intention is transformed directly into sound. They speak with a voice that is alive and connects directly with the life in us, the listeners. You might say that they use heart and soul as well as intellect.

Such vocal power is quite literally entrancing. Successful hypno-therapists use similar skills to influence their clients. Their deep soothing voice, working below conscious awareness, relaxes the client at a deep level to the point where they fall into trance. When it is time for the client to return to conscious awareness, the therapist's gradually brightening voice raises the client's energy levels and brings him back into normal waking consciousness. You too have the potential to influence others positively, to stir their being beneath their conscious awareness in positive ways. You have the power to motivate, empathise, galvanise and inspire, all by how you sound.

Chapter Three

Your voice tells a story

I speak Spanish to God, Italian to women, French to men, and German to my horse.

> attributed to the Holy Roman Emperor, Charles V

Are you happy with your voice? Or maybe that seems the wrong question, a bit like asking if you're happy with the size of your eyes. You may want to respond that whether you are or not isn't the point as there's not much you can do about it: your voice is your voice. You've got what you were born with. In fact, some people have one voice for all occasions, while others have voices that change all the time.

How is it for you? Does your voice stay broadly the same or does it change with different circumstances? In our house, I can always tell if my daughter is speaking to one of her friends or to her grandfather. The tone, pitch, speed and volume all change. She almost sounds like a different person on different occasions. The comedian Harry Enfield built a convincing comic character, the "super cool" teenager Kevin, on his observation of this phenomenon. When Kevin is speaking to his mates, his voice is rough and low. When, however, he meets a grown-up and feels less comfortable, his voice transforms into a tight, high-pitched squeak, "Yes, Mrs Jones, no, Mrs Jones."

Many people pick up traces of another person's accent when they converse. If your imitation is quite pronounced it can even be embarrassing! You might find that when you are speaking to someone who speaks slowly, you decrease your own speed or that when someone speaks to you in business-like tones you respond in a more clipped style. Listen to a mother turn from an adult conversation to respond to a child. The voice frequently becomes higher and lighter, and matches the child's tone beautifully, creating the warm link between them. When you are speaking the other person is likely to feel understood if your voice approaches the character and quality of theirs.

You might think it difficult to learn a different way of speaking but it can happen very naturally. My mother, from Lancashire, moved to Surrey before I was born and had a Surrey accent for the rest of her life. Her friend from the south moved up north to Cumbria and always seemed like a northerner to me. Was their change of accent connected with their willingness and desire to fit in to the local community, or did it happen subconsciously as their ear attuned to the new sounds? A bit of both, maybe.

Another family moved to the north of England from the Home Counties. The parents were very keen for their seven-year-old son to continue to "speak well", so they corrected his pronunciation frequently and he instinctively understood that only a certain kind of talking was acceptable at home. But at his new primary school the local children teased him on the very first day for his "posh" accent. So in no time at all he picked up the local pronunciation and began to match the other children perfectly while continuing to speak in his southern accent at home. In learning another accent for school, in a way he became "bilingual", with the two "languages" clearly demarcated in his mind. What is interesting is that he achieved this overnight. It is amazing what fears for self-survival can do!

You will know of other people whose accent remains strongly rooted in the place where they grew up. They can live a lifetime surrounded by people with a different accent and it doesn't affect how they speak one bit. There is the British person who goes abroad and has no concept of how to imitate the sounds of another language, while another traveller in no time at all begins to sound like a native.

We talk about one person having a good ear for languages and it is true that some of us have an enhanced auditory acuity that helps us to distinguish the more subtle variations in sound. It is also true that, through greater flexibility, less self-consciousness, or both, some people are more successful in adapting lips, tongue, teeth, palate and jaw to form unaccustomed sounds.

But these differences also have another story to tell, as we shall discover later. The way we speak, the way we change or do not change our accent and tone of voice when we speak to different people, the way our voice resonates and so on, have a reason and a purpose. There is nothing random about it. It all tells an important story. In fact, it tells *our* story.

My story – A tale of two voices

When I was about twelve, school came to an end for the summer, and I brought home my yearly report as usual. I handed it over without trepidation, as I enjoyed learning and liked competing in exams. On this occasion, my mother reacted with surprise when she reached the final general statement by the class teacher. It read, "Judy is sometimes very noisy and has a tendency to dominate her classmates by shouting over them." She stared, utterly astounded. At home, or around adults, I was the quietest person you could imagine. When adults were talking, I would often sit quietly in the room just listening without interrupting and would respond quietly when spoken to. Was this really her daughter? Well, yes, it was. With my friends, I was noisy and ebullient, and felt a wonderful sense of freedom every morning when I arrived at school. At home I was very quiet, usually with my head in a book.

By that time, though I didn't realise it then, I had acquired two distinct voices. The voice I used with my friends was loud and full of energy and laughter. The voice I reserved for those in authority was high and childish, gentle and biddable. These two distinct voices persisted side by side into adulthood.

It seems strange now that I was not aware of it for a long time. Yet, most of us are not very aware of the sounds we make when we speak unless our voice creates physical problems for us. We are too busy dealing with the content of our lives and the business of relating to others to take time to hear the actual sounds we are making, quite apart from the difficulty of actually hearing what we sound like to others.

I wasn't much aware of my voice again till in my twenties a musician boyfriend told me that I sounded different with different people. "It's strange," he said, "you have a strong voice when we are chatting together. But when we visit your family, it goes much higher and lighter."

That was another piece of the jigsaw but there was more to learn. I was studying singing and the spoken voice didn't seem to have much to do with that. Yet I was struggling with singing perform-ance. Almost every time I had a public singing engagement, I caught a cold just beforehand and felt tight and congested. When I sang on big occasions, my voice often narrowed so that I found the high notes challenging but equally struggled to get the lowest notes powerfully.

I had various teachers. One emphasised high and bright, and got me to sing more in "the mask", so that I could feel my voice reso-nate in my face. Another encouraged a rounder fuller sound, using lots of air. A third got me yodelling to "move the voice around". A fourth, who was a friend and helped me for free, encouraged me to make lots of different sounds and to compare the internal feelings of each—that was the most useful. Through a couple of sessions with him, having almost abandoned singing altogether, I began to observe and feel for myself. It was then that I finally had an "aha" moment, and made the connection between my spoken voice and my singing voice.

I suddenly realised that the voice I produced at auditions was the equivalent of my "biddable little girl" voice. No wonder it failed to move the audition panel: I was leaving half of myself behind, just as I did when I became the dutiful young person speaking to parents and other authority figures. The joyful, boisterous, fun and energetic self only came out when I chatted enthusiastically with my friends and felt entirely at my ease.

Through studying neurolinguistic programming I discovered the power of states of mind and how it was possible to change my state at will. I found that I didn't have to get stuck in an unhelpful state of mind. I could instead recall a positive state in all its colour and detail and feeling, and use that recalled feeling in the present whenever I needed it. All I had to do was to re-experience vividly those times when I was fully engaged with my friends and thus enter into that state and take on its physiology: relaxed shoulders, easy full breath and a feeling of energy. In that state, my voice was relaxed and resonant. This was a revelation, not only about voice but about myself as well. As you read this book, changing your state will be one of the ways that you can develop your voice too.

So my own journey continued. At that point I had made an important discovery: that the voice is a beautiful, blessed instrument for expressing who we are to the world, and that it can be a powerful instrument too, once we tune in to our full energy and being.

But let us go to the beginning and look back to the voice we were born with.

Your voice and your history

> Listen to his sound if you want to know a person.
>
> Dr Alexander Lowen, from *Bioenergetics*

The first of the five senses to develop in the unborn child is the sense of sound, many months before she[4] is born and begins to see. The foetus is aware of the sound of her mother's heart and voice at about six months and a bond is forged before they even meet. Sound is also the last sense we lose. We know that a dying person is aware of sound even after sight, touch, taste and smell have gone.

We have a life history of sound from cradle to grave and we carry through life our own vocal characteristics. How many voices are there? As many as there are people. The basic tone of your voice is like your fingerprint—gloriously, peculiarly you. Only, unlike your fingerprint, it can also change and develop, and therefore has the ability to express the person that you are today—if you allow it to. Just as your body shows life's "battle wounds" as you grow up—the odd scar, feet shaped by shoes and so on—so your voice is shaped by your history.

There's a book that I used to read every Christmas with my two children. At bedtime on Christmas Eve, when they both found it hard to contain their excitement, we would sit on the bed together and read *Lucy and Tom's Christmas* by Shirley Hughes. The precious ritual continued as a special part of Christmas several years after the children had outgrown the book, which had become well-thumbed and battered with almost every page telling its own story and receiving its comment year by year. "That's the page with glue on, from when we were putting glitter on our cards." "There's a jam mark where you were eating in bed." And the family joke: "That's the page which got a bit of your sick on it!" "It's not mine!" "Yes it is, don't you remember when you were two ...!"

Our voice is a bit like that book, with a piece of our history on every page. If we were hurt emotionally maybe we buried emotion, and warmth and feeling fell away from our voice. Maybe we discovered that being specially "nice" to people got us what we wanted, and our voice acquired a manipulative pleasant tone. Little by little our voice acquired its present characteristics.

Wilhelm Reich in the mid-twentieth century explored the concept of "character armouring", the way in which people, out of their conscious awareness, build up muscular tensions in the body to protect themselves against painful and threatening emotional experiences. He believed that in order to achieve full health it is necessary to eliminate this rigidity and pent up energy in the body.

Out of his work grew Bioenergetics, a therapy that helps people to regain their energy through releasing muscular blocks in the body. A fundamental thesis of the therapy is that what goes on in the mind reflects what is happening in the body and vice versa (and by body we can include voice). In his seminal book *Bioenergetics*, Alexander Lowen describes how emotional stress creates a state of tension in a part of the body which does not readily unfreeze again.[5] For example, an event which the child finds traumatic may tighten (freeze) part of his shoulder. When stress is chronic, muscular tension persists. This muscular tension decreases energy and restricts mobility, including the mobility of the voice. The restriction on the vocal apparatus restricts self-expression.

So your journey through life has affected your voice. When you were born, if you were healthy, you uttered your first sounds in a free cry emanating from your whole being. Then, when you learned to speak, the language itself moulded your use of your vocal apparatus, breathing, vowel and consonant sounds and tone. Even in a single language you can hear the different tones of the various native accents coming from different cultures. In English, for example, you hear the different tones of British, American, Canadian, Australian and other accents. Beyond this, your speech reflected your background, the time and place where as a child you first assimilated language in the particular accent, manner and tone of your carers, community, region and culture.

On your journey, emotional episodes have had an effect on your voice. Life events and traumas as you grew up inhibited the freedom of your body in various ways and the altered physiology affected your voice too. This starts very early on. Voice coach Patsy Rodenburg describes a sad visit to a battered baby unit, where the babies cry with voices that are already tight and restrained because of their life experiences.

As you continued to grow, if the behaviour of your carers constantly made you angry at the age of three, you may have muttered to yourself at the time through clenched teeth, "Just you wait till I grow up; I'll get my own back on you!" The anger, unexpressed openly, became lodged as a tightness in your jaw, which gave your voice a hard-edged quality. As an adult, this unresolved tension may still be lodged in the tone of your voice like unfinished business, though you may not feel as if you are still angry now.

Maybe as a child your voice was inhibited by adult chastising. This happens in many cultures. In British society, for example, language is full of phrases extolling quiet and calm as virtues: "children should be seen and not heard"; "silence is golden"; "empty vessels make the most sound". If you were told to be quiet or not to show off so often that you inhibited the exuberant part of yourself, it is possible that you lost access to the higher ranges of your voice where excitement and joy are expressed. If this is so, when you now want to express enthusiasm and exclaim for instance, "That was fanta-astic!!" or "So exci-iting!" your voice will not rise in pitch on the emphasised syllable. In fact, it will sound anything but exciting. This is a vocal problem I encounter fairly often in working with people.

Maybe you learned to guard what you say and the control has resulted in a monotonous tone. If, under stress, you try to establish a holding control over your voice, there is a loss of natural vibration and your voice will sound flat. One kind of lie detector functions by detecting flatness in the voice, so if you attempt to control your delivery in this way, you won't even sound truthful!

If you are always striving, the effort will show up as a habitual edginess to your voice however laid back you try to be. Stuttering is also likely to have its roots in tension, and studies to overcome stuttering have been successful through tackling this issue.[6] I have included some help for stuttering in the Appendix.

So, your current voice is an accumulation of the experiences you have had up to now. It expresses your energy, your state of mind and your sense of self. Your personality shows up in your voice.

The word "personality" derives from *persona*, the mask actors used to wear. But if you divide *persona* into its component Latin parts *per* and *sona*, you have the words *by* and *sound*. We know much about people by the sounds they make. When your voice is free your personality shines out as you speak. But on your life journey, through the various tensions of living, the sounds may have become constricted, and sometimes a person's voice is more like the mask that they hide behind. A discerning listener can hear that hidden story in your voice.

Voices that don't match

Have you ever heard someone whose voice just doesn't fit them? Maybe you meet a tall man weighing eighteen stones and when he speaks his voice is light and high? Or you hear an executive director speak at a conference and when she opens her mouth she sounds like a child? Really confusing!

Jill's voice surprised me when she first came to me for voice coaching. She was a highly motivated senior manager with a staff of about twenty-five. She frequently had to make presentations in various settings and seemed confident. But if you shut your eyes and listened to the high-pitched tones resonating from her head, you would think a child was speaking. And her voice never varied in quality, even when she challenged someone or showed irritation.

She was good at her job and seemed generally sure of herself, so her voice didn't fit her at all. Yet, certain factors in Jill's life went with the childish voice. She had great respect for authority and pleasing the chief executive was very important to her. She had a conscientious desire to "get things right". The rest of her life had a similar theme. She dutifully visited her elderly mother on her way home each day and listened to her minor complaints as she prepared a meal for her, before going on home to make dinner for her husband. Her motivation in all these positive actions was "to get things right". She was stuck in the role of pleasing others, and her voice also was stuck at that dependent child stage of development.

In essence, as an adult she was a divided self. The self she showed to the world was the dutiful, conscientious daughter/wife/senior employee. Her hidden self seemed far less "nice" to her and therefore felt better kept under wraps. However, the hiding was not completely successful as the unvarying nature of her voice revealed that something didn't fit. The tension involved in keeping her "less nice" self out of sight produced this voice that was too high and light for her adult frame.

When we worked together, simple voice coaching worked to a certain point, but convincing change demanded something more. She had to come to terms with growing into her adult voice on a psychological level as well as a physiological level before she was able to create the changes she wanted to make. When she began to assert adult independence of thought and action, and risk disapproval, her voice very rapidly began to deepen and grow in resonance. She reported that she felt much more at ease in her own skin too.

Nigel offers another example of a voice that didn't fit the person. He worked for one of the major international accountancy firms and was asked to do some work with a voice coach because it was suggested to him that his voice might present an impediment to promotion to board level.

His voice was high, tight and clipped, with a pronounced aristocratic accent. He was very tense in his demeanour too, and held himself with his shoulders fixed and high. Whatever was discussed, his voice remained strangled and firmly in his head.

In his case too, there was a link with his life. He was used to solving life's problems with his intellect and had done brilliantly up till now as regards study and career through using his brain. He had great respect for logic and reason, and was vehemently opposed to any validation of emotional intelligence, actively scorning what he called "touchy-feely" learning.

Anything that required his body to get involved was outside his comfort boundaries. Through his public school career he had covered lack of prowess at sport with speed of intellect. Feeling had also been protected in this way. If a fellow student teased him, he parried by being smart of tongue. Instead of being touched by life's sadness, he was used to adopting a stiff upper lip: "Life must go on."

So his body neither engaged in exercise nor was moved by feeling. Nigel was entirely cut off from motion and emotion, and so was his voice. He had no idea what it meant to give voice to feeling, or indeed, how feelings could be useful. At some stage in his life, he had made the decision, albeit unconsciously, to step out of feeling altogether. But without the energy of the whole body the true voice cannot speak.

Books on voice that deal with vocal technique (and are often aimed at actors) don't cover some of the aspects of voice revealed in these anecdotes. The journey of developing your voice goes beyond vocal technique to involve the whole of you. This makes finding your voice an exciting process—and even at times a daunting one—but one that can have rich rewards both in terms of how you communicate with others and of how you feel about yourself.

Let's first learn the basic sound-making process.

Part Two

What To Do
– The Basics

Chapter Four

Breathe!

Breath is the bridge which connects life to consciousness,
which unites your body to your thoughts.

Thich Nhat Hanh, Zen master

We are able to speak by a very simple process:

We breathe ...
　　we produce vibrations ...
　　　　which resonate ...
　　　　　　and we shape the words.

First we take in air, and the air flows under pressure, passing across the vocal cords.

The air causes the vocal cords to vibrate to make a sound.

We allow these sound waves to resonate in the mouth, nose and bones of the face and all the hollow spaces in the head, throat, chest and throughout our body. This amplifies the sound many times over.

Finally, we shape and articulate the sound as it emerges from the mouth by moving our jaw, lips, tongue and palate. Sound becomes intelligible as words and language.

It starts with breath

Breathing is the power mechanism for sending air across the vocal cords to make them vibrate, so it all starts with the breath. You breathe in and you speak. But how you breathe makes a huge difference, and the first important stage in uncovering your true voice is to learn to breathe more fully. That involves using more of your body when you breathe.

Breathing is a natural process that we all know how to do. We came out of our mother's womb and before we uttered full-throated sound for the first time we breathed! Even in tension we never stop breathing for more than a moment or two. Strangely, it's only when we stop to think about it that we can't remember exactly how we usually breathe. Watch someone when they are asleep. Their chest rises and falls naturally as the air enters the body and leaves again. The whole body is involved in the process in an easy gentle way.

Yet, the breath is one of the first things to be affected by trauma during the course of our life. In blocking our feelings, we block our breath. If you are with someone who is anxious and stressed, and you give them the instruction "Breathe!" you will see how their body suddenly unlocks itself as they take their first good breath for a while.

By the time you learned to speak, your breathing had probably already changed from that full breath you took at birth. For many of us, breathing becomes a shallow process that uses only the top part of the lungs, and certainly doesn't involve the whole body. At school, children used to be told to sit up straight, sometimes with rewards for those who did it most obviously. So those who ostentatiously pulled in the stomach and thrust out the chest won the prizes! You can still see young children do that if you urge them to sit up straight. If you try it, you'll find it constricts the muscles and hinders natural breathing. At least women don't suffer any longer the breathing constrictions of Victorian young ladies whose tight corsets used to be largely responsible for their tendency to faint in public.

Observe how others breathe when they speak. It is amazing how little breath some people take. Sometimes, you will see the upper chest rising and falling slightly as someone speaks, with perhaps a little movement in the shoulders, while the whole body below the level of the upper chest is inert. You can't take in very much air this way. Moreover, as the muscles used in breathing this way are not very effective in controlling the flow of air, the air tends to come out all in a rush. Someone breathing like that speaks in shorter sentences and tends to talk faster to compensate for the lack of air and muscle control. Sometimes the first thing you notice when such a person talks is how the speech pattern is broken up into lots of little bursts of air, often divided by non-verbal separators such as "er", "eh" and "um".

> "Oh, er … (breath) hello, er … (breath), yes, er … I'm very well thank you, um er … (breath) we've been eh … pretty busy you know (breath) eh, doing this and that er … (breath) … you know er …"

You might think this kind of speech indicates a muddled mind, but many speech hesitations are due to poor breathing. In order to control the air somehow, this speaker uses the muscles that are available high in the body in the upper chest, shoulders and neck, where the effect on the sound is to make it pinched and strained. All the little separators, the er's and um's, are caused by shortness of breath; they afford lots of little opportunities to grab another tiny quantity of air, and these snatches of air soon settle into an unconscious habit.

If you learn to use muscles lower down, especially the diaphragm, you'll get a much more robust tone and far greater control over the air. It can all be done easily and naturally. Many actors learn to exert strong control over the diaphragm and ignore the rest of their body. As a result, their voices sound strong but artificial and "manufactured". The best speakers, if they think about air at all, think of the involvement of the whole body.

Think of your breath as your good friend—which indeed it is. It has not let you down in all the time you have been alive: whether you have paid it attention or ignored it, whether you have been relaxed and happy or tense and upset, it has always been there with you keeping your system working. You can survive without food and water for days, but without breathing you would survive for only a very few minutes. So, as you breathe in, know that you can trust this friend, and enjoy the feeling of warmth and comfort that comes from moving the breath in and out.

So, let's take a breath

First, just be aware of your breath as you breathe in and out. Allow breathing; do not attempt to influence how you breathe.

Gradually, put your attention on relaxation as you breathe. Become aware of any areas of tension in your body and soften them as you breathe out. Be aware of how the breath moves the body, not vice versa.

Imagine a connection between your breath and the base of your spine, and sense the muscles all around your spine gently moving as you breathe.

Be aware of your inner vitality and of the breath's connection with it.

Next, you can deepen the breath ready for speaking.

Sigh of relief breath

You will take a better in-breath if you first get rid of the old air, so breathe out to empty your lungs. Breathe out in a relaxed way, keeping an upright easy posture. A good way to do this is to sigh with relief.

Think of a time when you felt a sudden sense of relief—when you heard the sound of the key in the door when a long-awaited loved one arrived home, for example, or when you received good news when you were expecting bad. Sigh with all the pleasure of relief. Feel how satisfying it is to get rid of all the stale old air.

As you breathe out, release each tension in your body as you become aware of it. During this process casually observe the involuntary in-breath that at some point replaces the sigh without any deliberate action on your part. The more you relax each part of you the more the in-breath will incorporate different parts of your body and be felt deep within. Remain standing in an open stance without collapsing your body around your chest.

This is the perfect breath for speech. The psychotherapist Stephen Gilligan in his book *The Courage To Love* uses the metaphor of God breathing air into Adam's nostrils in the myth of creation for effortless full breathing: "And the Lord God formed man of the dust of the ground, and breathed into his nostrils the breath of life; and man became a living soul" (Genesis 2:7). So, as you breathe out, you become ready to "be breathed into" by divine intervention, without your having to do anything at all. Have this image in your mind and just let it happen ...

Air from the centre of the earth

Here is another exercise to build awareness of good breathing. Stand upright with an open posture, body relaxed and shoulders wide. Breathe out and, as your lungs refill with air, imagine that the air is coming into you up out of the ground through the soles of your feet. Notice how the air feels fresh and seems to fill you from the ground upwards.

You can imagine the air coming up from the earth or you can imagine it streaming into you like golden oil as in the next exercise; whatever works best for you and gives you the full breath.

Air like a golden heavy stream

Breathe out again. This time imagine that the incoming air is a golden stream, as heavy as oil, which enters through your nose and pours into your elastic belly, filling the lowest part first. You may notice how the air feels cool as it enters your nose.

Try any and all of these exercises. They all use images, and one image will probably work better for you than another.

Good breath support

Make sure you are not making a big effort or tensing up as you breathe. When inhaling, your upper chest remains relaxed; your shoulders have no need to rise except gently in harmony with your lower body. Your waistline expands when you inhale and contracts when you exhale. Unless you are panting from exertion, this movement is small and almost imperceptible.

As an extra guide to feel the muscles used for breath support, place your fingertips just below your ribs and make a quick short cough. The muscles you feel contracting against your finger tips are the muscles you use for breath support. Breathing for good speaking does not require a lot of effort. If you generally feel relaxed and healthy you'll probably achieve a good breath quite naturally.

By the way, "breathing in" is a confusing term. When you breathe in, the only thing that goes "in" is air. Everything in your body relaxes and goes "out". You may feel your tummy moving out-wards, your ribs and other parts of your body expanding outwards to make space for the air. Welcome the air generously, and give it breadth and depth.

Join breath to sound

Once you have taken a good breath, you can use the air to make sound. Breathe out and take in air easily again. Then release the air into sound, counting from one to five out loud, slowly and eas-ily, enjoying the steady sound that emerges from a good breath. Allow each word to merge into the next one as you use the breath. Concentrate on the long sounds and just allow the breath to last as long as it comfortably can without any strain. If you do not reach the last number it does not matter. Do not be tempted to take a mini-breath in between one number and the next.

One-two-three-four-five.

Join the sounds together, so that they sound something like:

wuuu-ntoo-oo-threee-fooor-faaaai-v.

Just use the air you have without forcing anything, and move men-tally towards the last number as you speak.

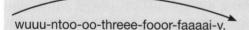

wuuu-ntoo-oo-threee-fooor-faaaai-v.

If you find that this lies well within your breathing capacity, then try breathing in and counting from one to six, or seven and so on. Your capacity will grow naturally in time.

Taking lots of air to speak doesn't mean that you will sound breathy. In the above exercise, every bit of air turns into sound, so you will have used all your air by the time you get to your last number.

Once you can do this exercise easily, you are ready to use your voice fully like an actor, so why not start straightaway with Shakespeare? His blank verse is just made for flowing breath.

Declaim Shakespeare

Speak the following in a joined-up way just as you did the number exercise, one breath to a line, and keeping up the energy to the end of each line. Declaim it strongly and enjoy the meaning of the words:

Shall I compare thee to a summer's day?
Thou art more lovely and more temperate:
Rough winds do shake the darling buds of May,
And Summer's lease hath all too short a date;
Sometime too hot the eye of heaven shines,
And often is his gold complexion dimm'd;
And every fair from fair sometime declines,
By chance or nature's changing course untrimm'd;
But thy eternal Summer shall not fade
Nor lose possession of that fair thou ow'st;
Nor shall Death brag thou wander'st in his shade,
When in eternal lines to time thou grow'st:
So long as men can breathe, or eyes can see,
So long lives this, and this gives life to thee.   Sonnet 18

To speak a longer piece like this successfully, you have to be able to take a breath after each line without interrupting the flow by taking too much time about it. The main thing is to stay easily upright with an open chest as your lungs empty of air, and not be tempted to collapse in your middle or chest as you get towards the end of your breath. If you stay open and stand tall, then as you release your diaphragm (relax your breathing muscles) at the end of the line, fresh air will readily flow into the space inside you. If you find yourself making heavy weather of taking in a fresh breath, it is probably because you have allowed your body to collapse. Allow yourself to use plenty of air as you declaim the verse loudly, and that will make the fresh breaths easier too.

This exercise will work best if you throw caution to the wind and declaim loudly like a great Shakespearian actor. Pretend you are an actor and have fun with it!

Chapter Five

Relax!

Don't underestimate the value of Doing Nothing, of just going along, listening to all the things you can't hear, and not bothering.

Pooh's Little Instruction Book, inspired by A. A. Milne

Good breathing is dependent on the flexibility and elasticity of the body. When you use your voice well you will feel relaxed, particularly around the area of the shoulders, neck and jaw. Your voice will sound free if your body feels free.

If you find that your voice does not project as much as you would like, tension is nearly always a major factor. It can feel counter-intuitive: you may feel that you have to push the sound out more forcefully in order to be heard, but the reverse is true. You need to relax more, to give your resonators a chance to ring. You will learn more about how to speak loudly in Chapter 8.

I possess a pair of Indian cymbals that I use to gain people's attention in courses. When you hold the metal tightly in each hand and clash them together, the resulting sound is a dead "tack" of metal against metal. But if you hold the cymbals loosely by their strings and touch them together, the ringing sound is surprisingly loud, travels far and always surprises people with its clarity, resonance and beauty of tone.

Your body is your resounding instrument, and like the cymbals needs to be free for the sound to ring through you. Relaxing your body releases your voice, and releases your mind and your whole being at the same time.

The opposite is also true. Tensing your body tenses your mind. Not only is your voice inhibited but your ability to listen is as well. You might have had the experience of tensing up with fear when you speak in public. When that happens, you hear your voice going tighter and higher in pitch, which is in itself anxiety-making, and your mind also becomes tense and unable to think clearly. Your "heart comes into your mouth". When this happens you can find yourself trapped in an escalating spiral of performance anxiety. When you release, you are more able to give out and to receive: you open up true communication. Be aware that relaxation is not the same as slump: there is still vital energy running through you.

Some tension in the body may be the temporary effect of a stressful day or too much time spent hunched up before a computer screen. Some tension however, as we have seen, is habitual, a result of holding yourself in a particular way for years, often from childhood, as a defence against life's traumas.

In *Bioenergetics,* Alexander Lowen cites three areas of obstruction to the voice. The first is the mouth which prevents the inner self from expressing itself by being clamped shut with compressed lips and tight jaw. The second is the junction of the head and the neck where we swallow. This area guards against being forced to "swallow" anything unacceptable and against any feelings being expressed that may be unacceptable. The third is the junction of the neck and the thorax which guards the opening to the chest and the heart, and so prevents feelings from being expressed audibly.

These obstructions are physical but were installed by mental tensions. You can unblock them by relaxing physically *and* by addressing the mental obstacles. Mind and body are inextricably linked. This connection demonstrates itself beautifully when, as you learn to relax parts of your body that are accustomed to being tense, some of your life problems and blocks also begin to drop away.

So relaxation has much going for it, and especially with regard to the voice. So let's find ways to release tensions in the body.

Posture, physiology

> How beautiful it is to do nothing, and then to rest afterward.
>
> Spanish proverb

Being at ease starts with how you hold your body. If your skeleton is unbalanced, that will put tension on certain muscles, and therefore affect your breathing and your voice. If your structure is aligned and balanced, it provides the support that your voice needs. Good posture also adds to your personal confidence and gives others the sense of your assurance and authority.

Stand tall and admire the view

Stand upright and balanced evenly with your feet about hip-width apart and pointing forward. Feel the contact of your feet with the soles of your shoes, and through them to the floor.

Stand tall, with your head level and your shoulders relaxed. Keeping your head in this position as if hanging in the sky, release the rest of your body and let it hang so that every vertebra of your spine is hanging down from the one above. Remember to release your knees as well. Be aware of the width of your back. Feel the relaxation spread right through you.

Within that relaxation, feel alive in every cell. Breathe in and feel yourself fill the space in the room.

As you stand there, imagine that you have climbed to the top of a hill and have just come over the summit. Open your chest to breathe in the fresh air as you see the open expanse of land and sky stretching out before you.

See the view, feel the fresh air and breathe it in … quiet, peace and wide expanse …

Now try this light-hearted approach to relaxation which can be extremely effective.

Model "laid-back"

As children, we learned some of our most important lessons by imitating and this process can serve us well as adults. Find someone who you find very relaxed or laid-back. Now spend some minutes imitating this relaxed person. (Ask a friend if you can use them as a model or copy someone on the television.)

Imitating means that you act as if you are the other person. It's like "trying them on". The key is to notice as much as you can about how they are in that relaxed mode and then to embody it. Stand in the same way, balance in the same way, hold your head and shoulders in the same way, move and gesture like them, breathe like them and then speak in the same way.

Spend several minutes doing this—if your model is a friend, you could for instance go for a walk and a talk with them. What are the main differences from your habitual way of being? You may for example find their stance is very different from your habitual one and makes you feel different, and of course speak differently. There are many ways of being in this world!

It's a good idea to practise relaxation at many moments during the day. Even if you are busy, two minutes out of your life will make a positive difference. Thousands of us have work patterns that keep us sitting at a computer for hours at a time, and our bodies get locked and tense. Get into the habit of taking a mini-break to move every now and then. This can be as short as two minutes, and you don't even have to move from your work station to perform the movements.

Take a two minute movement break

Look up from your screen, and if possible swivel your chair away from sight of it. Take a good breath in and blow all the air out with a "phew" sound, letting your shoulders fall at the same time. Repeat.

Drop your head down towards your chest and then gently backwards.

Turn your head to the right and to the left a few times. If it is quiet around you, you may hear a healthy creaking sound in your neck as you unwind the tension.

With your head facing forwards, move your right ear towards the right shoulder and then your left ear towards your left shoulder. Repeat a few times.

Very gently, make a complete circle with your head, down, around to the left, up, around to the right and back. Then make a circle in the opposite direction.

Circle your shoulders forwards both together, backwards both together and then individually backwards and forwards. Again, you may hear the bones creak!

Release your jaw and your whole face, including your tongue. Feel the tension drain away from your cheeks. Move your jaw up and down and gently from side to side. Put your fingers behind and below your ears and gently massage the back of the jaw.

Rub your palms vigorously together to make them warm and then cup the palms over your relaxed open eyes to cut out all the light. Hold them thus for ten to twenty seconds.

Finally, look up, breathe in and feel the air cold in your nasal passages. Release the air again. Repeat a couple of times. Be aware that every cell in your body is alive and feel energy in every part of your body.

And here's an even shorter meditative relaxation exercise. Get someone to read this short relaxation script to you, or record it and play it back to yourself, so that during the minute you can just sit at ease with your eyes closed. This is a good one to record for your mobile phone and earphones. Do it a couple of times a day, maybe in the morning and again in the evening. When you record it or read it allow generous pauses between the sentences.

Try the one minute all-over relaxation exercise

Find a quiet space where you won't be disturbed, and begin.

Sit comfortably and gently close your eyes. Now lift your eyelids just to the point where they might open but don't, and then release them again. Relax the muscles around your eyes to the point that your eyes just don't work. Imagine that your eyelids are so relaxed that they just don't work. Try them out to make sure. Now allow that relaxed feeling to spread smoothly down through your body right to your toes—spreading gently right through you down to your toes. Now feel your arms completely relax. The hands and arms will be just like a heavy wet cloth. If someone tries to lift an arm it will be like a heavy wet cloth and will just flop back into your lap. Completely relaxed like this. Now this relaxation spreads to the whole of you and you feel yourself melting, dissolving in a sensation of ease and relaxation and peace. That's right.

After a few moments silence, begin to move and stretch, be aware of your surroundings again and finally open your eyes.

You may be surprised at how far you can lose yourself in peace and quiet in such a short time. It's good to remind ourselves that we don't need more time to relax. We just need intention and the right state of mind.

If the parts of your body close to the vocal folds are free from tension your voice has the flexibility to resonate fully, so your throat and jaw require particular loving attention.

Relax your throat

Sit comfortably and close your eyes. Let the tension drain from your body and try to fall asleep.

Now yawn, and open your throat as you do. (You will feel the soft palate go up and the back of the tongue go down.)

Let a deep *Aah* sound come out. Repeat a few times.

Gently sit up and open your eyes.

One more exercise, for your jaw this time. The jaw is amazingly strong: it is capable of exerting 3,000 pounds of force per square inch. You may have seen or heard of trapeze artistes who hang or support great weights from the jaw. It can also hold much psychological tension and present a fearsome constriction to the free voice. People sometimes hold a load of personal history in a stiff jaw.

Relax your jaw

Try this exercise for loosening the jaw and releasing the voice:

Open the mouth wide suddenly as you look down (as if you have suddenly spotted a creepy crawly on the floor!). Relax.

Open the jaws wide suddenly and look up (as if you have spotted something amazing in the sky!). Relax.

Repeat several times.

This exercise is especially useful if you speak in an accent that naturally encourages you to clench the jaw.

Free flow

> The human voice is the organ of the soul.
>
> Henry Wadsworth Longfellow

These exercises to release tension are particularly important for the voice because when you relax your body, your voice is able to do what it naturally wants to do, which is to resound freely. There's such a difference between a voice that resounds and rings, and a voice that is forced and pushed! One sounds harsh and dead, and the other expresses the full richness of your communication. Moreover, allowing your voice to resound freely does more than just release the sound of your voice: it allows your voice to connect with what is going on for you mentally and emotionally.

The great theatre director and teacher, Jerzy Grotowski, always told his students that the voice emerged from the physiology: "The *body* must work first. Afterwards comes the *voice*," he insisted. "Before reacting with the voice, you must first react with the body. If you think, you must think with your body."[7] When there is freedom in the body, your mere intention in speaking will create natural vibrations in different parts of the body and your voice will naturally express in sound everything that you wish to communicate of your human intelligence, energy and spirit.

Chapter Six

Let your voice ring!

Two Voices are there; one is of the sea,
One of the mountains: each a mighty Voice.

William Wordsworth, "Sonnet to Liberty"

So, we have learnt that relaxation is fundamental. And when you relax, your voice is free to resonate naturally and create rich and varied sounds. Your voice resonates in many different parts of your body at the same time, and the most influential speakers make full use of the varied sounds created by resonance in different parts of the body to communicate their meaning. Your impact as a speaker will depend on how you use the natural resonance of your head and body. It's most likely that you use some resonators more than others, and you can develop your voice so that the underused ones work better for you.

Different resonators create different effects. Their impact will become clearer as we proceed but I will mention their effects briefly here. The high sounds that you make when the vibrations resonate in your head project energy and excitement; chest resonance has the ring of authority, maturity and trust; the lower sounding heart resonance communicates feeling and passion; and, lowest of all, gut resonance expresses fundamental truths. They work together—in different proportions at different times—but let's look at each individually first to clarify their effects and uses.

Head resonance – excitement, carrying power

A baby is an alimentary canal with a loud voice at one end and no responsibility at the other.

Jerome K. Jerome

I live near a school and if I am in the garden when it's the children's play-time, I hear the high-pitched sound of young voices letting off steam. Last week was sports day and the sounds were even higher than usual, as the children shouted excitedly for their teams. If you have ever been to a rock concert you will be familiar with the high-pitched sounds of excited people, whether child or adult.

The high voice that resonates in the head has two important functions: it shows energy and excitement, and it carries well. People with natural enthusiasm and vitality tend to speak at a higher pitch, and certainly raise the pitch so that it vibrates in the head at moments of excitement. For example, if they exclaim, "It was fan**tas**tic!" the pitch goes up high for the accented syllable.

Head resonance is also an important component in your ability to project, when used together with other areas of resonance, but more of that later.

We also sometimes use just the head voice without the stronger resonances of the body when we speak to children, and it can be associated with gentleness and caring.

You might think that the high head voice doesn't belong in a serious speech or a conference setting. But great speakers make effective use of their head voice, to add light and shade to what they say. They just don't stay up there all the time.

So how do you produce these high sounds? There are various ways. Be ready to play. Realise that these high sounds are only going to be a small *part* of your repertoire of sounds to create a varied interesting voice. But they are a vital part.

Producing the head voice

Start by making a long whOO-OO-OOP! sound that starts low and quiet and quickly whizzes up as high in pitch as you can, getting rapidly louder and ending suddenly. The last part of the sound will be your head voice. After a few repetitions of "whoop", repeat the highest part of the sound on its own: whOO-OO-OOP! then, OOP!

Listen to the cartoon characters on children's television programmes and imitate the way they speak. You'll find a variety of different head voices there.

Imagine your voice coming lightly from the middle of your head. Experiment with directing the sound into your nose, your cheeks or the top of your head. Sense the voice issuing from your ears. Make cat sounds, squeaky mouse sounds, shrill bird sounds—have fun experimenting.

Imagine you are calling a dog back across a wide field in a high carrying singsong voice on the notes sung by the cuckoo: "Fido!" (Fiii-Doo!). Call loudly so the dog can hear you!

Think of something you did that was exciting—yes, you can think of something! Hear the excitement in your voice when you allow parts of a word to hit the high head voice, like for instance the second /æ/ sound in the word fantastic. Think of what you did that was really exciting, and then say with great enthusiasm:

"That was fan-**taaaa**-stic!"

Choose your own word for expressing enthusiasm (e.g. amazing, awesome, splendid, fabulous, tremendous). How high can you make the sound go on the stressed syllable? Just get genuinely excited and it will happen. You may have to feel quite childlike!

Now contrast that with the following. Speak these phrases all on one tone, emphasising the syllable in bold, but not allowing the pitch to slip higher or lower in pitch:

"That was absolutely a**ma**zing"
"What a fan**tas**tic offer"
"That's a **bri**lliant suggestion

Notice the difference!

Down-side of the head voice

If you speak just using head resonance and nothing else, you can sound strident or childish. Some head voices also sound devoid of feeling, like an over-intellectual professor or an "anorak". The head voice is a wonderful aspect of your full voice, but needs the other resonances to give your voice variety and sound its best.

Especially for women

A woman's high voice can impinge particularly strongly on the ear. Hillary Clinton has sometimes been accused by the media of having a shrieking high voice. Of course, it is all too easy for journalists to attack a woman in public life for being strident, hectoring, shrill, shrieking or the ultimate insult, unfeminine. On other occasions a woman with a gentle high voice is accused of sounding childish or weak. It can sometimes seem that women in public life cannot win as regards the voice.

Perhaps for this reason, women in public life often work to cultivate a lower voice. Former UK Prime Minister Margaret Thatcher was sometimes accused in her early years of the tendency to shriek in the House. Later, she learned how to speak in the artificially deep voice which became her hallmark. Now, women in business and politics are increasingly working with a voice coach to learn how to adopt deeper tones.

As a woman, you can learn to make more use of the lower resonances described below without losing the essential quality of your voice or the ability to vary your voice. The head voice is essential as part of your toolkit if you want to convey genuine enthusiasm and energy. The skill is to have access to that resonance and then use it as appropriate.

Moderation in lowering your voice helps you to maintain different resonances and therefore variety. If you lower your natural pitch too drastically, you risk vocal fatigue, hoarseness and a sore larynx. Your voice has a natural pitch to suit your body shape and weight, and you will feel most comfortable if you speak within that range. We will come back to this again when we talk about speaking with confidence in Chapter 9.

Throat resonance – permission to speak

My voice stuck in my throat.

Virgil, *The Aeneid*

When someone close to you talks fairly quietly you can hear the sound resonating in the area of their throat. When we speak louder, this resonance is no longer sufficient and we need to use more body resonance to avoid forcing the voice.

Do you sometimes feel the need to clear your throat when you have to talk in public? Or your throat feels constricted? Tension in the throat is one of the first symptoms of anxiety. Nerves make you tighten up around the shoulders as you draw yourself in for protection, and this causes the voice to become higher and tighter. When you hear this happening to your voice, you may fear loss of control and feel even more anxious, and a vicious circle is created. We are back to learning how to relax …

If you have any difficulty in projecting your voice, the throat is usually the place where you sense an inhibition. This can be the effect of the anxiety of the moment but can also be due to chronic tension. If you have built into your psyche certain imperatives, for example, "Never cry", "Don't sing, you sound awful", "Stop showing off", it is quite likely that this presents itself physically as a block in your throat, preventing you from being spontaneous. If then you wish to voice sorrow, joy, laughter or anger in a spontaneous way, you may find that the ability is no longer accessible to you, until you teach yourself how to again.

Sometimes, just an indefinable low level fear holds you back. It may be a sense of, "I can't" or "I'm not good enough". This feeling of being blocked at the throat is in our language: "He felt choked up", "There was a lump in her throat", "The words stuck in her throat", "He felt gagged".

Giving yourself permission to express yourself from your throat literally means "to find your voice". Releasing your throat feels like giving way to more expression of yourself on the inside, and will certainly increase your range of vocal expression on the outside. It can also be accompanied by the release of emotions that were hidden to you before.

Mary's story

Mary never felt she counted in her family. She was an "after-thought", the child born years after her family with two older siblings was "complete". She remembers how she was aware as a young child that she held the rest of the family back from exciting outings on holidays by not being old enough to manage the activities. A very quiet child, she always sought to fit in with the wishes of the rest of her family as much as she could.

Mary always had problems in getting herself heard. In middle life, she went on a voice course and successfully recovered her voice from all the tension around her throat. She cried as she rediscovered her voice. I asked her what made the difference during the course, and she replied, "It was discovering that I had the right to be me."

"I never realised that I had a right to exist," she confessed. "And now, I know that I do!"

Open the breathing channel

Just drop your head easily back, open your mouth and stick out your tongue, and breathe in and out with your mouth in the "aaah" position. Feel the direct connection between the sky and your breathing place in your belly (diaphragm) without the throat getting in the way. Now say "haaa" as you breathe out, and feel how the sound comes right up from your body. After a few times, move your head back to its normal position and repeat the "haaa", maintaining the same feeling as before.

Opening the door of the throat

Imagine that there is a double door located at the back of your neck in the throat area which opens towards the front of your throat. Take a slow inward breath, and as you do so, imagine this door at the back of your throat opening towards the front of your throat. Then when it is fully open, and you are full of air, then express that openness in sound as you expel the air. Say "Ye-e-e-es" with warm feeling, or some other affirmative words. Notice the warm quality of the sound. Your throat should stay soft throughout.

If this exercise gives rise to feelings within you, welcome them with your new voice.

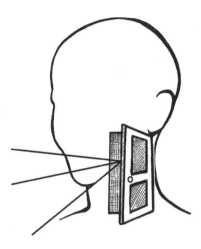

The throat sits at a point between the heart and the tongue, and acts as a doorway between feeling and speaking. In the Eastern tradition of chakras, the throat is connected with permission to speak, the ability to fearlessly express your truth, to be heard and understood. It is also sometimes called the "will centre".

The throat functions well when heart and mind are in tune with each other, and this happens when you express yourself with integrity. Any expression that is not internally truthful violates this centre. For example, if you speak calmly (from the head) when you are feeling upset (in the heart), or even don't speak at all when you are feeling angry, you block the healthy working of this part of your body. You may have experienced a lump in the throat when you don't know how to say what needs to be said in a situation, and push down emotion. When this happens repeatedly you lose the elasticity and openness of the throat, and the free voice is blocked.

When you succeed in opening up your throat, your voice sounds much more energetic and alive, and other people pay more heed to what you say.

Chest resonance – authority, maturity, trust

Speech is power: speech is to persuade, to convert, to compel.

Ralph Waldo Emerson

There is a long, flat bone down the centre line of your chest—the sternum. This sets up a strong resonance when you are convinced and determined, and when you express something that your intellect holds to be true. This voice sounds grown-up, confident and purposeful, and people tend to trust it.

Listen to recordings of Sir Winston Churchill, Bill Clinton or Mary Robinson, the ex-President of Ireland: their tone of voice gives weight to what they say. You hear the voice of a man or woman who makes decisions firmly and moves things forward. On the other hand, if someone makes a determined statement and it resonates in a different place—in the heart for example—most people intuitively know that the speaker is not unwavering, but rather seeking approval or consensus.

Former UK Prime Minister John Major always struggled to convey confidence and gravitas with a voice that resonated quite high in the throat and head. The sound coming from a tight throat certainly did not act in his favour, even after voice coaching. He was often attacked in the media for wavering and uncertainty in his decision making, and his voice accentuated the impression in people's minds.

Listen for the chest voice in politicians and other leaders, and listen for its absence. If you listen to recordings of Tony Blair as Prime Minister, you will hear that, although he does use this voice on occasions, he is more at home with enthusiasm and with speaking from the heart. When he makes pronouncements that he knows to be unpopular his voice often fails to resonate in the chest but resonates a bit higher and tighter, and we find ourselves not quite believing him. If you contrast his pronouncements during the Iraq conflict with the war-time speeches of Winston Churchill, you will hear just how reassuring that deep chest resonance of Churchill is.

Producing the chest voice

Hold your hands at chest level, gripping tightly an imaginary jar with a broad lid, and try hard to unscrew the stiff top, making the sound of effort in your chest: "Agh!" Then say words from the same place.

Talk about something you have a strong opinion about, or are convinced about, with strong emphasis. If you are truly confident about your right to hold that opinion your voice will resonate in the chest area. You literally "get things off your chest".

Some people find it easier to find the resonance at first if they express a strong opinion about something they *don't* like or things they think ought *not* to happen. Accessing a feeling of anger can help. Think of something that really annoys you, and speak strongly about that, using such phrases as:

"It's *very wrong!*"
"It *shouldn't* be allowed to *happen*"
"I *hate* it when ..."

Then in an emphatic voice, without being angry, speak about something you have a firm, positive opinion about. If you are concerned about other people's opinions of your views, you will find it hard to do. This voice of conviction doesn't change whatever others' views might be.

Imagine someone has deliberately trodden on your toe, and say "Ouch! That hurt!" or "Stop that!" indignantly.

A good way to release this resonance is to beat your chest and make Tarzan sounds. Find a place where you can make loud sounds without inhibition and let go!

When you produce this resonance successfully, you will be able to feel the vibrations in your chest when you place a hand there whilst speaking. This is a strong voice and good to listen to.

Even this resonance however will become monotonous if it is not varied from time to time. It especially needs the contrast of the voice of feeling.

Heart resonance – feeling, caring

> Her voice is full of money.
>
> F. Scott Fitzgerald, *The Great Gatsby*

> His voice was as intimate as the rustle of sheets.
>
> Dorothy Parker

The voice of the heart wins hearts as well as minds. This is the voice of emotion and passion, the voice of feeling. It can be warm and caring, loud and desperate, joyous or excited. The tone is usually quite low and has a soft edge and natural vibration to it. This voice connects directly with the emotions of others and draws them into what you are feeling. If you speak with feeling your voice will naturally resonate around the area of the heart. This voice connects directly with the feelings of your listeners and literally captures hearts.

It is impossible to create this resonance authentically unless you have direct access to the emotion yourself at the very moment you are speaking. If you do not "relive" the emotion, the voice does not resonate naturally in this heart place, simple as that. A politician might try to fake it from time to time, and speak in a low voice with a passionate tremor when he proclaims a belief in "this grea-ea-ea-t na-a-a-ation" or "free-ee-eedom for a-a-all". You can usually tell the difference!

Once you have created rapport with another person or a group of people, this tone of voice more than any other will exert influence. A compassionate leader motivates through capturing people's hearts and minds, and shows understanding and empathy. Listen to the great leaders of our time and former times: they speak from the heart and *move* their listeners to action, that is by touching them emotionally. They are literally *moved*.

However, many people have lost this ability and live permanently at one remove from their emotions, like James Joyce's character Mr Duffy in "A Painful Case", who "lived at a little distance from his body, regarding his own acts with doubtful side-glasses".

Access to this voice is sometimes lost when someone continually pushes down unwanted feelings. This was the case with Jo. She was someone who seemed to have a zest for life and a good sense of humour, but her voice was cultured, metallic and monotonous. Sadly for her, people were put off by her voice.

As I got to know her, I discovered that she had been married for twenty years to a husband who was a bully and relentlessly put her down. Yet Jo did a remarkably good job in keeping up a full-time job and running a home without help. She told me that as a child too, she had been the one to keep things together while her two siblings got into drugs and trouble. The whole family had depended on her reliability from an early age and she had assumed the role. "Duty" was a word used often in her childhood home.

Jo's voice expressed in sound a persistent tension in her shoulders, neck and especially jaw. Jo didn't realise how angry she was, at the impositions made on her as a child and the treatment she endured now. A young child who has no vehicle to express anger hides it in the body where it becomes a chronic rigidity. Jo's anger locked in shoulders and jaw robbed her voice of its free vitality. Her journey to finding her voice involved getting feeling back, including anger. Only then was she able to give genuine expression to feeling in her voice and express more of herself.

Producing the voice of the heart

So, to speak from the heart you need only get in touch with real feeling and allow it to be heard. The energy of feeling is perhaps the most important thing to find if you want your voice to come alive.

Think of somewhere you love to relax and just be, and sigh, "Mmm …" with the pleasure of the memory. Or remember the hedonistic feeling of tasting your favourite food and make a similar sound, "Mmm …" Then add a sentence in the same tone: "Mmm … I love it here …" "Mmm … that tastes so good …"

Focus on your heart and speak warmly about something you truly care about or feel emotional about: a place, a person, an animal, an activity, an object of beauty. Allow yourself to connect with the feeling and express how you feel. If you usually exert a tight hold on your emotions, this will involve some letting go.

The sound is very different from the sound of enthusiasm. This voice is about letting go, *allowing* yourself to enjoy a memory or thought and simply giving expression to that feeling of enjoyment. Speaking from the heart is literally that: resonating from your heart.

Both the chest voice and the voice of the heart are used to express things that matter to you. If they matter to you in the sense of belief, thinking and opinion, the chest voice will naturally be engaged. If they matter to you in your heart—in other words, if you love them or care about them—the words will naturally resonate lower, in the area of your heart.

Gut resonance – fundamentals

There is no index so sure as the voice.

Tancred

When your whole being is engaged, your voice resonates deep in your body. This happens when all parts of you are committed to what you have to say. There is a low voice used by highly influential people which everyone listens to, because it comes so surely from the whole person. It is the quiet voice of intuition, the voice that captures a deeper felt truth, and it carries with it an authority that is instantly recognised and acknowledged.

Imagine a noisy meeting, and then a voice is heard to say quietly something like:

"Go for it."

or, "It won't work, let it go."

or, "That's it. That's the answer."

Everyone turns towards the voice as they hear its quiet certainty. It is the voice of a leader in tune with himself, which carries the ring of authority. People talk of "a gut response". When you speak from this place, you will find that the deep body resonance will slow down your speech and add to the gravitas of your communication.

Producing the gut voice

This voice uses the deepest resonators and feels as if it comes from your whole person, every fibre of your being.

Stand upright and relaxed. Hum gently and quietly in a deep tone, allowing the sound to vibrate through your whole body. You may like to use the sound, *Aum*. Be aware of the vibration through your body. You may feel a tingling in your arms, hands, chest, back or other parts of your body. With this same sensation/vibration, quietly introduce your spoken voice.

Think of a time when you were very certain about something, and after all the arguments had been made, something just had to be said. It might have been a short phrase such as: "But, we've got to do it", or "That's it, we're finished", or "Go for it". Allow your body to relax right down, and just say the words in a low voice.

Think about your deepest purpose. Ask yourself the question, "What's it all about?" "Why am I here?" Find that place deep within you where you can respond with truth. Settle down into your body, relax and hum in a quiet low voice. Feel how your whole body vibrates with the deep sound. That is the voice of the gut. Think of something you hold as a truth from your deeper purpose, and give it voice.

"I believe in peace."
"Respect—that's my deepest value."
"That's my truth."

What is it that needs to be said? Say it in that low voice.

The intuitive leader listens to the inner voice of wisdom and follows its deep instinct. This voice is more often associated with maturity than with a younger person. It is the missing piece of leadership after you have learned all the active skills. It belongs to *being* more than to *doing*.

Gut voice and hypnosis

Each kind of resonance can exert influence. The excitement of the head voice can enthuse people. The strength of the chest voice can convince. The feelings of the voice of the heart can move people. The voice of the gut connects on a deeper, quieter level. These sounds lack the conscious awareness of excitement, intellectual energy or emotion. They operate at the level of instinctive know-ing. When someone speaks with this voice from deep inside them it resonates inside the listener on a similarly deep level, and the sensation for the listener is almost that the voice comes not from outside but from inside their own body.

This then is the voice for putting someone into trance. The deep sounds float into the other person's consciousness and the sensa-tion is that they arise from inside. Connection is made mainly at a level below conscious awareness.

As with every other resonance, it is quite possible to imitate the voice of the gut by speaking in a low, soft-edged tone. But the best practitioners of hypnosis operate from a deep knowing and connection, and the voice influences the other person at that level, allowing them to trust and relax.

Resonance and communication

Your voice does not lie. It reveals much more about you than you might imagine. If you want to be effective as a communicator and as a leader, you need to speak from your whole truth, and this means using all parts of your voice: the positive energy and enthusiasm of the head voice, the determination of the chest voice, the compassion of the heart voice and the wise intuition of the gut voice.

Most people have some tension in the voice and therefore their voice does not resonate freely in all parts of their body. Some people as we have seen have almost no access to a particular resonance and this coincides with lack of access to the personal qualities associated with that vibration. To give a few examples:

The inhibited person has no head resonance and usually little resonance in chest, heart or gut either. The voice tone seems to come in a constricted way from around the neck and throat.

Someone who has not fully grown up, who lacks conviction or whose self-image is as son or daughter more than adult, or pupil more than teacher, for example, may have a voice with predominant head resonance, which sounds childish or immature.

Someone who is over-intellectual, like the stereotypical college professor, whose focus in life is confined to logic and rational processes with an avoidance or ignorance of emotion, will have a tighter version of the immature voice, with resonance in head and throat and no deeper tones.

A dominant personality, who masks the expression of feeling and lacks the ability to laugh at herself, will speak entirely with strong chest resonance and lack access to the softer tones of the heart and the bright sounds of head.

Someone who cares excessively what others think and finds it difficult to take a stand against the opinions of other people will lack the resonance in the chest that would give his sound confidence and conviction.

The renowned writer Arundhati Roy provides an example of someone who uses the whole voice. When she speaks up against the powers that be, to support the poor and oppressed, her voice comes from the whole of her, and thus inspires the listener.

The whole voice—that is, one that resonates subtly and naturally in head, chest, heart and gut to express the person fully—is difficult to fake. You can hear it in people of any age: in the open and natural voice of a young person or in the sounds of wisdom and maturity that are the fruits of long life experience.

Summary of kinds of influence

Head voice – enthusiasm

> *"I'm excited"*

The listener is carried along by your energy and excitement.

Chest voice – conviction

> *"I mean what I say"*

The listener believes you, senses your certainty.

Heart voice – love, caring

> *"I speak as I feel"*

The listener is moved by what you say, is led by your passion and full-hearted commitment.

Gut voice – the whole person

> *"I say it as it is"*

The listener is carried along with you. Your speaking resonates through your whole body. Your single-minded intention makes things happen. Your energy, coming from the whole of you, is a powerful attractor. The listener believes that whatever you want will happen.

Use your whole body for listening too

Just as it is possible to speak from the whole person, so it is possible to listen with the whole person. People who are most intuitive in coaching and helping others tend to listen not only with their ears, but also open their heart and gut to the sound of the other person's voice. This concept of listening with all your being is captured beautifully in the Chinese symbol for "listen". It consists of five sections: the whole left half denotes the "ear"; the right half is in four sections: at the top is "you", under this is "eyes", below that is "undivided attention" and at the bottom "heart".

When you listen from the whole of you, you begin to hear more of what is going on for someone, beyond the actual words. You then find that what is actually said is only the surface structure of the communication. The deeper truth lies beneath and you can hear it in the sound of the voice beyond the words: the sadness beneath accusation, the anger beneath righteousness, the hopelessness beneath complaining and the vulnerability beneath insistence.

Whole body, whole being

> The best voices engage the heart, the mind and the body.
>
> Richard Eyre, former artistic director of
> the Royal National Theatre

Speaking from the whole person eventually becomes an out-of-conscious skill, like driving a car. Once you have access to all the available resonators in your body and can express yourself fully, then you don't need to think about particular resonators: it all happens quite naturally as you breathe and speak with intention. When you become more animated, your voice naturally rises in pitch; when you express emotion, your voice naturally has the soft edge of heart resonance; when you express a strong belief, your voice rings out from the chest. This is something entirely different from "putting expression" into your delivery. One is a feeble prettification of what you are trying to say; the other is vital, alive, powerful and remarkably complex.

Every sound possible for a human being can be available for self-expression: laughing, crying, convulsing, singing, cheering, shouting, screaming, shrieking, giggling, laughing, wailing, purring, cooing, calling. How many sounds do you allow yourself to express? What are the voices of your emotions that perhaps you do not let out in public? Perhaps not in private either? What *is* the voice of your private moments—the voice of letting go?

Your repertoire of sounds

Find a private space and experiment with sound. How many of your sounds do you allow the world to hear?

The more you have access to the full range of expression, the greater becomes the possibility to communicate with others in a meaningful way.

Your personality is revealed more in your voice than in any other part of you. Your authentic personality shines out when you allow the free flow of the sound in your body, and produce the full range of richness.

So give your voice a workout! Shout! Sing!

Chapter Seven

Speak clearly!

We have looked at three of the four elements of voice. When we have learned how to breathe, relax and amplify our vocal cord vibrations with resonance we can make reverberant sounds. Now there is one final element which turns the sounds into communication.

Sound does not become speech until we form it into words. Whatever you say, however loudly or quietly you say it, the aim is to be clearly understood. To be understood you need to pronounce your words clearly: that is, articulate.

Articulation consists of moving your jaw, lips, tongue, teeth, soft palate and facial muscles to form the shape of the words. Freedom is again the key concept, for these parts of our body need to be flexible and agile enough to translate our thoughts and feelings into speech. Your mouth forms the shapes of the vowels and these are punctuated with consonants to make the sense. The exercises for you to try below do not depend on your adopting a particular accent: the criterion for success is always that you be clearly understood by your listeners. This requires mobility in all parts of your face. If you are used to speaking with a tight jaw, this will feel very strange. Some of us move these parts of our body so little when we speak that we would make fine ventriloquists!

Give yourself a warm-up first. Move your mouth, lips, jaw and teeth vigorously, stretching in all directions, making "funny faces".

Consonants – clarity and emphasis

Mobility work-out

The more relaxed you are around the jaw, lips, mouth, tongue and palate, the better you will articulate and the clearer you will sound.

Let's start with the lips: imitate a horse whinnying by blowing out with your lips loosely together, making a "Brrr" sound. Try the same thing with a "Whrrrr" sound and a "Prrrrr" sound. The lips should vibrate freely as well as the tongue roll on the /r/.

Now for the jaw: say the following fast and energetically, keeping your jaw very loose and the vowel sounds clear. Stick to a rhythm, two beats to each line.

```
1 ---------^--------- 2 ---------^---------
```
Bee-bee-bee-bee bee-ee-ee-ee (to rhyme with "see")
Beh-beh-beh-beh   be-e-e-e-eh (to rhyme with the vowel sound in "said")
Bah-bah-bah-bah ba-a-a-ah (to rhyme with "car")
Boh-boh-boh-boh bo-o-o-oh (to rhyme with the vowel sound in "hot")
Boo-boo-boo-boo boo-oo-oo-oo (to rhyme with "do")

Use lots of energy, but at the same time relax your facial muscles.

The relaxation exercises in Chapter 5 are also useful here.

Voiced consonants

Some consonants are produced entirely by the use of tongue and teeth, without engaging the vocal cords to make the sounds. Examples of these are /t/, /p/, /k/, /s/ and /f/.

Practise producing them entirely with tongue, teeth and breath, without voicing a sound: you will just hear the explosion of air released by the consonant.

Unvoiced consonants

Each one of the above consonants has a voiced counterpart produced with the same movement of tongue and teeth, this time engaging the vocal cords:

Voiced sound (using vocal cords)	Unvoiced equivalent (using breath without vocal cords)
/d/	/t/
/b/	/p/
/g/	/k/
/z/	/s/
/v/	/f/

It is very easy to mishear these similar sounds, so you need to make sure they sound different from each other. Try saying one and then its partner quite quickly one after the other. You will notice how you always need to engage the vocal cords to say the voiced consonant and explode a little bit of air to say the unvoiced consonant: /p/, /b/, /p/, /b/ and so on.

Now practise short nonsense sayings that use both voiced and unvoiced consonants:

Consonants workout

Putty butty, putty butty, putty butty
Cat gut, cat gut, cat gut
Pretty kitty, pretty kitty,
Kipper, kitty, kipper, kitty
Fast van, fast van, fast van
Ted the dentist, Ted the dentist

Long consonants

/D/ and /t/, /b/ and /p/, /g/ and /k/ are short plosive consonants that need to be crisp and clear. Other consonants can be lengthened, which gives the word additional emphasis:

/m/   **Mmm**arvellous
/n/   **Nnn**ever
/f/   **Fff**abulous
/v/   **Vvv**ast
/s/   **Sss**oft
/z/   **Zzz**enith
/w/   **Www**onderful
/r/   **Rrr**adiant
/sh/   **Shshsh**ame
/h/   **Hhh**orrible

Consonants are not just about clarity. They are also a vital means to express yourself more powerfully. You can make particular words stand out by lengthening the consonants on accented syllables or, if the consonants are short, by giving them additional emphasis.

First the long consonants.

Long consonants workout

Try saying the words listed above in full sentences and feel the effect of stretching out the consonant much longer than usual with great expression. For example:

"That was an absolutely **mmmmm**arvellous concert!"
"Please **nnnnn**ever do that again!"
"We drove across **vvvvv**ast open plains"
"That was the most **hhhh**orrrrible experience"

"**Hhhh**orrible!" The actual sound of such a word when emphasised reinforces the sense in a most satisfying way.

Short consonants workout

With short consonants, say them very clearly with sharp emphasis so that the word really stands out:

"**D**on't go near the water!"
"It was a **t**errible waste"
"Thanks so much—this is **p**erfect!"
"This way is so much **b**etter"

"It left a **g**aping hole"
"Of **c**ourse we'll help!"

Tongue twister workout

The English language has many examples of little poems and tongue twisters that play on consonants and provide challenging practice for exercising your lips, teeth and jaw.

Try reciting a few of the following to increase your clarity and flexibility! You will need to keep your jaw, your lips, your tongue and your teeth mobile and relaxed. Start slowly and then increase your speed.

A big black bug bit a big black bear, made the big black bear bleed blood.

Brad's big black bath brush broke.

Copper kettle bric-a-brac.

Crisp crusts crackle crunchily.

Double bubble gum bubbles double.

I correctly recollect Rebecca MacGregor's reckoning.

Knife and a fork, bottle and a cork,
that is the way you spell New York.

Lovely lemon liniment.

Mrs Smith's Fish Sauce Shop.

One smart fellow, he felt smart.
Two smart fellows, they felt smart.
Three smart fellows, they all felt smart.

Peter Piper picked a peck of pickled peppers.
Did Peter Piper pick a peck of pickled peppers?
If Peter Piper picked a peck of pickled peppers,
Where's the peck of pickled peppers Peter Piper picked?

Red lorry, yellow lorry, red lorry, yellow lorry.

Sam's shop stocks short spotted socks.

There was a minimum of cinnamon in the aluminium pan.

Three grey geese in the green grass grazing.
Grey were the geese and green was the grass.

Toy boat, toy boat, toy boat.

Which wristwatches are Swiss wristwatches?

Good consonants are an important key in bringing your speaking alive, as we shall expand later.

Recite in silence

A fun way to improve your pronunciation of consonants is to mouth a speech without sound. You will find that you automatically use your facial muscles far more than you would in normal audible speech. Whisper the following passage very clearly, allowing the release of air but not voicing any sound. It might surprise you how your facial muscles start to ache when you really work out!

"Is there anybody there?" said the Traveller,
Knocking on the moonlit door;
And his horse in the silence champed the grasses
Of the forest's ferny floor.
And a bird flew up out of the turret,
Above the Traveller's head:
And he smote upon the door again a second time;
"Is there anybody there?" he said.

Try whispering other pieces of text, from a newspaper for instance. Give it a rest whenever you feel yourself tense up. Your voice muscles enjoy a workout just like your body but, as with going to the gym, you need to build up the flexibility gradually.

You might like to do the exercise as a game with a friend. You mouth sentences or numbers to each other and see if you can understand each other by lip reading alone.

Vowels – feeling and emotion in the voice

The vowels are the singing part of the voice and the main vehicle for feeling and emotion. When we give the vowels more space and length our voice begins to sound much more interesting.

Lovely long vowels

We have already looked at the impact of long consonants. We can greatly increase the impact of what we are saying by now lengthening long vowels in key words, for example:

fo-o-remost
fan**ta-a**stic
nee-eed
lo-**o**ng
dema-**a**nd
trans**fo-o**rm

Lengthen vowels for expression

Try out some of these words in sentences. If you can feel an emotion or energy that fits the words while you are saying them, you'll find it easier and the effect will be even stronger.

"We **nee-ee**d to move **fo-or**ward"
"The dema-**a**nds are **la-ar**ge"
"The rewa-**ar**ds are fan**ta-a**stic"

When you start to enjoy vowels, you can capture the sense of a word in all its meaning. Think of a word, like "generous" for example. Get a real sense of the meaning of generosity: its amplitude, its richness, and put all that meaning into the first vowel sound, "**ge-e-e**nerous" — a generous sound! Discover the determination in the second and fourth syllables of "de**te-e**rmin**a-a**tion" as you speak the word firmly. It is a fun process to use the consonants and vowels of any word to express its meaning. Find some words that have resonance for you and say them in a way that uses the sound to emphasise the meaning. Remember that you can lengthen both vowels and consonants. Here are a few to start you off:

---

gentle
catastrophic
enormous
slippery
heavy

Vowels and consonants and emphasis

The clear vowel sounds we have practised so far are important for the emphasised words in a sentence. Correct English pronunciation uses quite lazy vowels on unaccented syllables. You can often tell speakers who have *learned* English as a second language because they tend to pronounce every syllable with accurate vowels. Native English speakers do not do this.

Take the phrase, "I want to go". If you say the sentence at conversational speed, you will not pronounce "to" with the vowel "oo". Instead it will become /t/ with a hiatus, or the sound "ter". The secret of dramatically improving your pronunciation is to make beautifully clear vowels on the *main accented* syllables. This allows words that are important for the meaning to stand out strongly, like images in sharp focus against a less distinct background.

Try it for yourself by reading a short piece from a newspaper. You will find it sharpens the impact of what you have to say. It does not of course mean that you slide over the words in between.

Clear thinking and articulation

Successful articulation is only partly physical. There is a strong psychological element too. One of the main enemies of good articulation is muddy thinking. If you are uncertain or constantly changing your mind as you speak, or thinking of alternatives and caveats as you go, it is easy for your speaking to become hesitant and unclear. When you learn to think clearly "on the hoof", you will find that it helps your fluency too.

Articulation is sometimes half-hearted because the speaker is unsure whether she really wants to be heard or not. You also need to want to be heard.

Part Three

The How Tos – Common Questions Answered

Chapter Eight

How can I get other people to listen to me?

The next few chapters offer some immediate remedies for the kind of voice difficulties I meet most often. You can dip in and read the sections that most interest you. You will find tips and suggestions that are readily and easily applicable for tackling particular voice issues.

One of the most common problems raised by coach clients is, "People just don't listen to me. I don't know if my voice is too quiet or whether it's to do with my personality, but I feel ignored half the time." This is often a cry from the heart: "Why am I ignored? What is it about me that makes me so easily passed by?" Getting other people to listen to you is not just a practical communication skill; it also has great rewards in terms of your self-perception and self-esteem.

So how *can* you get people to listen to you?

Be clear and audible!

Let's start with the obvious. If people can actually hear and understand what you are saying they are much more likely to pay heed to what you say. People will listen to you only if they can receive your message with the minimum of effort. When you speak in a group and get no response you may feel ignored and rejected, but the truth may be that other people just have not heard or understood you. People can feel awkward about constantly repeating, "I'm sorry, can you say that again?" every time you open your mouth, and eventually will stop asking you to repeat yourself and just give up the effort to understand.

So what is needed for you to be clear when you speak? Firstly:

73

Slow down!

Speed has a major effect on impact. In films, a scene is sometimes speeded up for comic or frantic effect. A scene that is slowed down often has a powerful heroic impact: you sense the epic triumph of a film hero as his best moment is screened in slow motion. Slowing your words has a similar effect. Think of how some of the memorable phrases of our politicians were delivered:

* The phrase of President Obama's election campaign, "Yes, we can".
* Margaret Thatcher's "The lady is not for turning".
* Winston Churchill's "We will never surrender".

So, to sound authoritative and effective, slow down. But don't grind to a halt!

Talk at a pace that is easy to follow, neither too fast nor too slow. One way to practise this is to try the following reading exercise.

"Look and speak" exercise

Choose part of a speech or a newspaper article to read. Look down and breathe in, reading the first phrase silently. Then look up and speak the words you have just read. Again look down, breathe in and read. Then again look up and speak.

The rules of the exercise are: when you are speaking you must look up; when you are looking down to breathe and read you must stay silent. Try it out with this excerpt from one of John F. Kennedy's speeches:

But peace does not rest in the charters and covenants alone. It lies in the hearts and minds of all people. So let us not rest all our hopes on parchment and on paper, let us strive to build peace, a desire for peace, a willingness to work for peace in the hearts and minds of all of our people.

That speech might divide as follows:

[Breathe and read the first phrase.]

But peace does not rest
[Look up and speak it. Breathe while looking at next phrase.]

in the charters and covenants alone.
[Look up and speak it. Breathe and look at next phrase.]

It lies in the hearts and minds
[Look up and speak it. Breathe and look at next phrase.]

of all people.
[Look up and speak it. Breathe and look at next phrase.]

So let us not rest all our hopes
[Look up and speak it. Breathe and look at next phrase.]

on parchment and on paper,
[Look up and speak it. Breathe and look at next phrase.]

let us strive to build peace,
[Look up and speak it. Breathe and look at next phrase.]

a desire for peace,
[Look up and speak it. Breathe and look at next phrase.]

a willingness to work for peace
[Look up and speak it. Breathe and look at next phrase.]

in the hearts and minds
[Look up and speak it. Breathe and look at next phrase.]

of all of our people.
[Look up and speak it.]

You will find that the breathing/reading pauses seem absurdly long unless you slow down your speaking speed to compensate. So work on taking reading pauses that fit in with the speed of your delivery, and you will find yourself naturally slowing down. With a really steady speaking pace, the reading gaps will seem just easy breathing pauses in the steady flow of your words.

If you are reading a speech, you may like to lay it out on the page with a separate line for each breath as I have done above. This helps you to find your place easily when you glance down.

Proclaim in a big voice

We have already used a passage from Shakespeare to work on breathing. Here is a soliloquy from *Julius Caesar* for you to practise measured speech. Proclaim the blank verse in a big voice, joining the words one to another in dramatic declamation. See how slowly you can speak it and still hold on to the sense of grandeur:

Why, man, he doth bestride the narrow world
Like a Colossus, and we petty men
Walk under his huge legs and peep about
To find ourselves dishonourable graves.
Men at sometime are masters of their fates.
The fault, dear Brutus, is not in our stars,
But in ourselves, that we are underlings ...
Now, in the names of all the gods at once,
Upon what meat doth this our Caesar feed
That he is grown so great?

Use plenty of breath, speak out confidently and loudly, and imagine you are a great actor in a large space.

Now, as yourself, introduce yourself to an imaginary audience in similar tones! Try it out on a friend and ask for their response. My guess is that they won't find it as exaggerated as you will!

Speak clearly!

The second essential for being heard is to make sure that your vowels and consonants are really clear. Have a look again at the previous chapter to remind yourself how to do that. Read the Julius Caesar speech again and this time make the most of the long consonants, the short sharp consonants and the long vowels, all in bold. Have some fun overdoing it!

> Why, **mmm**an, he **d**oth be**sssstri-i**de the **nnn**arrow **wwwo-o**rld
> **Lll**ike a **Colll**ossus, and **wwwe-e** petty **mmm**en
> **Www**alk under his **hhhu-u**ge **lll**egs and **pee-ee**p about
> To **fffi-i**nd our**sss**selves **d**ishonourable **grrra-a**ves.
> **Mmm**en at **sss**someti-**i**me are **mmma-a**sters of their **fffa-a**tes.
> The **fff**ault, dear **Brrr**utus, is **nnn**ot in our **sssta-a**rs,
> But in our**sss**selves, that **wwwe-e** are under**lll**ings ...
> **Nnno-o**w, in the **nnna-a**mes of **a-allll** the **g**ods at once,
> Upon what **mmmea-ea**t doth **thththis** our **Cccae-ae**sar **fffee-ee**d
> That **hhhe-e** is **grrro-o**wn so **grrrea-ea**t?

Learning to emphasise like this will really improve your public
speaking in a very short time.

Exaggerate the words

Now, with the reasoning that to achieve 100% on the day you need
to be able to achieve 120% in practice, try a quote from Dylan
Thomas's *Under Milk Wood*. Throw yourself into a flamboyant exag-
geration of vowels and consonants. If your accent comes out Welsh,
all the better, for it helps the flow!

And the shrill girls giggle and master around him and squeal as
they clutch and thrash, and he blubbers away downhill with his
patched pants falling, and his tear splashed blush burns all the
way as the triumphant bird-like *sisters scream with buttons* in
their claws and the bully brothers hoot after him his little nick-
name and his mother's shame and his father's wickedness with
the loose wild barefoot women of the hovels of the hills.

Take what you have learned from these texts and apply it to your
own words. Record your voice and then play it back. I would guess
it won't sound as exaggerated as it feels. And that is an important
clue to improving your clarity. It's very possible that you think you
are overdoing it when you are not at all ... which leads us on to the
next point ...

Project your voice in making presentations

Do you know how loudly you actually speak? Most of us don't and some of us fear that we are speaking too loudly when others find us scarcely audible. We are not always the best judge of how loudly we are speaking. We have already noted that you are bound to sound louder to yourself because you are hearing your own sounds from the inside, echoing around all your lovely bone structure.

The other week, a sceptical participant turned up to the second day of one of my courses clutching a decibel meter to measure the sound of people's voices. He just didn't believe that he spoke quieter than other people. We all tried out the machine and then he conceded defeat: "Well, you're right," he admitted. "I do speak quietly. I would never have believed it. It sounds so loud inside my head!"

Getting heard is not *just* about increasing your volume but it is certainly useful to be able to speak loudly in order to be heard against background noise when you need to. How do you do that?

Volume requires good breath and freedom around the shoulders, neck and jaw. So the first thing in practice is to limber up and do some relaxation exercises. (See examples in Chapter 5.) If your body is free of tension, and provided that your vocal cords are healthy and you use good breath, the voice will ring out: it can't do otherwise. Don't believe it?

Jump and shout

Find a place and a time where you can make a noise without inhibition.

Limber up and get yourself in a relaxed and playful state, where you don't mind what result you get.

Jump in the air and, just as you land, completely synchronised with the sound of your feet hitting the floor, shout loudly, "Haa!"

Try this several times. Do it together with someone else. If you have some fun with it the results will be even more striking.

You will be surprised at the volume you produce when you remove your voluntary control over your voice in this way.

Here is another way to achieve a similar effect:

Shake and shout

As in the exercise above, find a place and a time where you can make a noise without inhibition.

Limber up and get yourself in a relaxed and playful state, where you don't mind what result you get.

This time, instead of jumping, shake your whole body vigorously: your arms, shoulders, body, waist, hips, legs and knees. Make sure that you do shake all parts of your body, head, arms and legs—some people seem able to shake while keeping head, neck and torso completely rigid, which is not the idea!

As you shake your body, release an energetic long "Aaaaaaah!" Hear how the shaking of your body frees up the sound.

Now, say a couple of sentences with lots of expression while shaking up and down as before. It seems like a childish exercise, so how about reciting a nursery rhyme?

Baa, baa, black sheep, have you any wool?
Yes, sir, yes, sir, three bags full.

Allow the sound to come out just as it wants to.

Shout and greet

Imagine you suddenly see someone you know across the street, shoot your arm out in a greeting and as you do call out, "Hey!" to get their attention. Hear the sound come right out from the centre of you.

Do it again, and say a bit more this time: "Hey! Thomas! Come and join us!"

It might surprise you in the above exercises that *when you really let go*, you have a big voice. Any lack of volume is likely to be due to your attempts to control the voice, not your lack of voice (unless you have some physical problem with your vocal cords). So the secret of projecting your voice is to let go, not to push the sound forward. This is one of those cases where your instinct doesn't always help. You might feel that you need to try hard, to push the voice out to force it to sound loud, but the more physical effort you use, the less effective you will be.

Speaking loudly doesn't need a big physical effort but it does require strong intention. If you are ever shocked into yelling loudly in an emergency you never have the time to think about whether the voice is loud or not: it just is! However, it is an amazing but sad fact that often people's sense of inhibition is so strong that even in a genuine emergency they are unable to shout. Children in some cultures have to be taught to shout in an emergency in order to break through their taught "civility". So you need to have a strong intention to be heard; and then you will be.

In public speaking the goal is usually to be heard without shouting: to project rather than yell. Professional speakers often speak of "placing the voice". When you are in a large space, imagine that you are placing your voice into the farthest corners.

Place your voice

Hold your hand just in front your face, and say "Hello, pleased to meet you" to it.

Look at a point half-way across the room, and repeat the phrase, placing your voice at that point with a feeling of an arc of sound reaching the spot.

Look at the farthest corner of the room, and repeat, placing your voice further in a larger arc.

Look at a distant point out of the window, and repeat, placing your voice far into the distance in a high arc.

Hear how the voice changes, creating more and more high resonance to travel the distance. Remember to breathe well as you do it.

Project waves of sound

Think of the sound as waves emanating from your body in all directions, from your back as much as from your mouth. This encourages you to use your whole body, and not to force the sound forwards. Think of yourself as a pebble falling into a pool of water, and the sound spreads out in a circle around you in all directions.

81

Feel the vibration in your back as you speak. Think of the sound emanating from the back of your head towards the ceiling behind, from between your shoulder blades straight backwards, from the small of the back backwards and from the bottom of your spine towards the floor a distance behind.

Then think of the top front of your head projecting the voice towards the ceiling in front, the mouth placing the voice in front of your face, the throat gloriously open allowing the voice straight outwards, the chest outwards and the belly sending the voice towards the floor. Focus on each part of your body in turn and have fun projecting your voice from each. The sound spreads in all directions like the light from a lighthouse.

Speaking quietly and clearly requires strong intention too. If you wish to make a point quietly it is a good idea to think of every aspect of your voice as being large—apart from the volume. So use plenty of breath, enunciate the words with clear vowels and consonants, and be aware of a strong intention to be heard. Then your quiet speaking will be listened to and have impact.

Good speakers lower their voice to draw the audience in and raise it to make a point.

Women and projection

> Her voice was ever soft, Gentle and low, an excellent thing in
> woman.
>
> Shakespeare, *King Lear*

If you are a woman you face a long history of stereotypical taboos
about how you should and shouldn't sound, and you may have a
fear of sounding like a harpy if you raise your voice to be heard or
of sounding piercing or shrill if you speak up at a meeting. Once
you learn to use body resonance as well as head resonance, as we
spoke about in the last chapter, this is no longer a problem.

Even if you think your voice is too high pitched, it does not help to
force your voice low and loud. That will cut you off from the ability
to express variation in your voice and also put a damaging strain
on your vocal chords. Your voice sounds best within its normal
range.

Fill the room mentally

Projection is a vocal skill; it is also a state of mind. If you fill the
room mentally, your voice is likely to follow.

Gesture and space exercise

Stand tall and relaxed, with an open posture, hands hanging freely by
your sides, well balanced on both feet, as you have practised before.
As you breathe, have the sense that you are filling the space of the
room or auditorium. This is *your* space and you have the inner energy
to fill it mentally. Feel every cell in your body alive.

Imagine that one arm is the shaft of a light sabre and that brilliant
light is pouring out of your fingers towards the floor. Raise your hand
slowly and feel your fingers with light pouring from them sweep
slowly across the floor to the base of the far wall, slowly up the wall
and right up to touch the corner of the ceiling.

> Experience how that gesture is grand and large enough to fill the space, and appreciate how you need to stand and be in that space to match that kind of gesture.
>
> Be aware of your vital energy filling the room and reaching the people you wish to communicate with before you even open your mouth. If you practise this gesture slowly and mindfully in different rooms you will sense the different energy required to fill different spaces.

This is definitely an exercise you need to perform physically to get the learning from it.

Think big! As Nelson Mandela said famously in his inaugural presidential address in 1994:

> Your playing small doesn't serve the world. There's nothing enlightened about shrinking so that other people won't feel insecure around you. We were born to make manifest the glory that is within us. It's not just in some of us; it's in EVERYONE! And as we let our own light shine, we unconsciously give other people permission to do the same. As we are liberated from our own fear, our presence automatically liberates others!
>
> Marianne Williamson, quoted by Nelson Mandela

Vary your delivery! Sound more interesting

You will be much more interesting to listen to if your speech is varied. Even a confident energetic speaker can become boring if she carries on relentlessly. Most of us can cite tedious examples of conference presentations where the speaker was clear and audible but never varied the tone or paused. Have you ever seen a baby sound asleep in the midst of a din? We can do that too. If the sound of a voice is constant it can easily send people to sleep even when it is loud and clear.

Ex US President Bill Clinton is a good example of a speaker who varies his voice. His voice is not particularly deep but he engages his audience by varying his delivery constantly.

Do *you* sound monotonous?

Monotony test

Make an everyday statement, for example. "Can you pass the salt please." Now adopt the same tone and level (i.e. pitch) of voice for the following statements:

"What a fantastic day!"

"I believe strongly in fairness"

"I'm passionate about my country"

If you find it normal for your voice not to change to make widely differing statements, then monotony is a potential problem.

There's a simple answer to the problem. If you want to avoid sounding monotonous, *vary* your speech in every way you can. If you listen to the great speakers, their delivery is constantly varied in pitch, tone, speed and volume. They use clear vowel and consonant sounds to aid understanding and to enliven what they say. They use different rhythms. They use silence to punctuate their speech. They emphasise some words more strongly than others to bring out the sense of what they say. They vary the language they use, so that it is not all abstract expressions but includes the language of the senses.

So how do you vary your voice?

There are so many ways to introduce variety! The vocal wheel reminds you how many different ways there are. Avoid being predictable. People like the element of surprise, and it keeps them attentive.

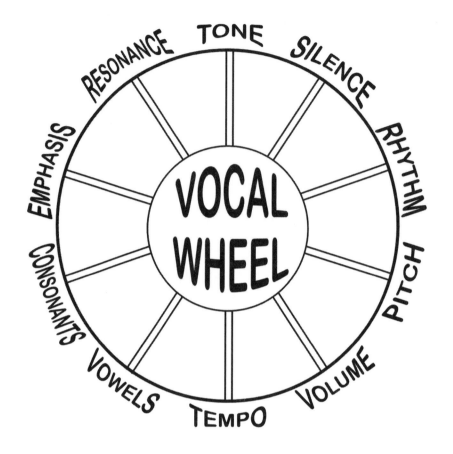

Resonance

Remember all the different resonances. Speak from head, heart and gut to make different points.

Tone

Sometimes your voice can sound smooth and mellifluous, at other times it can sound rougher and grittier.

Silence

Allow silent spaces now and then to allow people to process what you are saying and to regain their attention to make an important point. Sometimes it is also good to pause and to listen, to give people a moment, to WAIT:

Why
Am
I
Talking?

Rhythm

Think of speaking as if it were music, and vary the rhythm of your phrases. Great speakers do this all the time. Repeat the rhythm of a phrase, then change it. Churchill in a wartime speech repeated the patterns of, "We shall fight on the beaches, we shall fight on the landing grounds, we shall fight in the fields and in the streets, we shall fight in the hills." The change of rhythm in "We will never surrender" creates a strong impact on us.

Pitch

Vary the highs and lows of your voice. Allow your voice to go up and down naturally. Pitching your voice at different levels will give what you say much more interest. Use your whole instrument.

Volume

It is monotonous to have to struggle to hear someone who is mumbling; and it's just as dull to listen to an unwavering booming tone at a steady volume. So vary your volume control as well. Speak loudly sometimes to gain attention or create an impact. Then say some things softly to draw people into your circle and make them listen attentively in a different way. This of course requires the ability to speak loudly and softly when you want to.

Tempo

Do you hurry over your words or do you talk slowly? To make an impact, you need to be able to vary the speed of your delivery. This depends partly on good breathing so that you have enough air to slow down when you want to. Good articulation and emphasis also help to slow you down and increase intelligibility and interest for your listeners. Slow down to make a memorable point. Perhaps speed up to tell an anecdote.

Vowels

Use the long vowels to bring out words that have a strong emotional charge.

Consonants

Strong consonants make a strong impact. Use them when you want to stress a point.

Emphasis

This is a great way to bring your speech alive. Emphasise the key concepts and the words essential to the sense. If you have some information that you really want people to remember, slow it down, say it clearly and accentuate it. You can always speed up a little for some of your narrative, provided that people can hear clearly what you have to say.

Recite your own 'Boom' poem

Here's a challenge. Practise varying your delivery, by reciting a 'Boom' poem, inspired by the television comedy programme, *Blackadder*. In *Blackadder Goes Forth*, the series about the First World War, the character Baldrick recites a couple of his own war poems.[8] The second one goes thus:

Boom! Boom! Boom! Boom!
   Boom! Boom! **Boom!**
   Boom! Boom! Boom! **Boom!**
   Boom! Boom! **Boom!**

He declaims his verse in a loud, relentless voice, devastating in its dreariness. But here is the challenge: make it interesting, even with such impoverished material! You can enliven it by putting passion, excitement, tragedy, comedy, sadness, happiness and every other emotion into it. See how many emotions you can express in a single line. It might be fun to have a contest with a friend.

Boom! **Boom!** Boom! Boom!
Boom! Boom! **Boom!**
Boom! **BOOM!** *Boom!* **Boom!**
Boom! Boom! **Boom!**

Vary your language

Finally, vary the kinds of words you use. Don't use entirely abstract language; also use words that people can see, hear, touch and feel. Read the following passage which employs abstract language and apply your monotony sensor to it:

> A comprehensive transitional integrated framework strategy, responsive to logistical considerations and dedicated to the optimisation of organisational mobility will enhance overall global programming and the functional capability of interactive management units providing a state of the art systemic paradigm fit for all contingencies and planning projections.

A high monotony count, I think!

If you look at famous old speeches you will find that they are full of words that paint pictures, sounds and movement. Take a couple of sentences from Martin Luther King's famous, "I have a dream" speech:

> I have a dream that one day every valley shall be exalted, every hill and mountain shall be made low, the rough places will be made plain, and the crooked places will be made straight, and the glory of the Lord shall be revealed, and all flesh shall see it together … Let freedom ring from every hill and every molehill of Mississippi. From every mountainside, let freedom ring.

He creates images that you can see, hear *and* feel.

Be heard in meetings—mismatch sometimes

If you have had the experience of being ignored at meetings, you may need to learn how to express yourself differently. In general conversation, we tend to talk in a similar way to each other, at about the same speed, volume and so on. If you want to be noticed, break this pattern: *do something different.*

If everyone is talking loudly, and you talk loudly, you won't be noticed. If everyone is talking fast, and you talk fast, you won't be noticed. If you always interrupt others with your views as a matter of course, you won't be noticed.

Speak in a way that contrasts with the general hubbub; in other words mismatch—at least to gain entry into the conversation. You may have to raise your voice just for an instant to be heard at all, but then quickly move into contrast mode, and you will be amazed how people will notice your voice as you begin to speak.

Use your whole voice

Have you ever been in a situation similar to the one described in the Prologue of this book? You have tried to make a point in a meeting and created little impact, only to have the idea picked up with enthusiasm a while later when someone else says exactly the same thing? Frustrating, to say the least! The person who is listened to in a meeting is often the one who uses his lower resonance more than others and speaks at a firmer, slower pace. If your voice resonates low in your body it will cut through in a way that even a strident or shrill voice will not. Look at the section on gut resonance in Chapter 6 for how to do this.

If your first couple of words come from that place you will catch people's attention. You can then pause for a moment, or repeat the words, so that you have everyone's full attention before proceeding.

The following section, on believing yourself, is also important here. Believe in what you are saying and others will take it on board.

Believe yourself, keep yourself interested

Carol came to me and said she had received feedback that her presentation style was flat. She wanted to learn how to sound interesting when she gave her bi-monthly report at the board meeting. "So, what *is* interesting about it?" I asked. "Oh, it's deadly dull!" she responded. "Then", I replied, "you are being wonderfully authentic."

If *you* are not interested, if *you* don't believe it, why should other people? This doesn't mean that you have to find a subject fascinating in order to connect with interest. It does mean you need to find a way to make the exercise worthwhile for you and everyone else. Ask yourself why you are putting any point across. If you have no answer to the question, then perhaps you shouldn't be doing it by means of a speech, and everyone will thank you for saving their time.

You may indeed be interested but think that others cannot possibly be interested in what you have to say. Know why you are speaking, what you want to communicate, why it matters to you and what you want to achieve. This is all about self-belief and courage. If you are passionate about something and can allow that passion to become visible, others will catch your passion. Believe in what you are saying and others will be drawn into it too. Take the last two sentences; try them out—*as if they were true*—and see what results you get.

This is about honouring yourself. Get involved in what you are saying, use your energy and natural humour, give *yourself* a good time, and other people will be drawn in as if by magic. This is a skill that you can practise at any time, with friends, family, anyone you feel relatively comfortable with.

One of my coaching clients who regularly delivered the company's financial figures to the board found it hard to maintain people's interest. So he made mental pictures from the figures to bring them alive for people: "Our profits have reduced this month by 'x' amount," he said. "Do you realise that is the equivalent of half the homes in Liverpool going without heating or lighting?"

Another client was describing the interest rates for particular investments in Europe. Originally, he just quoted the figures: England is so much, France is so much, Sweden is so much, and on and on. He revised it thus: "Go to Sweden!" he announced. "In Sweden, you are going to find a bargain! The rates are so much. Now contrast that with the UK, where such and such applies ..." Instead of a list, he created a story, a hook on which to hang the figures.

Build high intention and energy

The big question in getting listened to is, "Do you really want to be heard?" And for many of us the answer is, "Yes, I do and no, I don't." Yes, I want to be heard, but I'm not certain that I can cope with the attention I might receive if I am heard. Or, yes, I want to be heard, but the best people are seen and not heard. Or yes, I want to be heard, but then people might find out that I have nothing of note to say ... and on and on, with many doubts and worries about being heard.

When you become certain that you want to be heard, you will be heard. And this means building high intention.

What do you really want when you open your mouth to speak? What do you want to communicate? What is the purpose of your opening your mouth? What matters about it? What do you want to say that expresses your own values? As you are able to answer these questions, you will begin to clarify your intention and build your energy around it. If you then release this energy into words, other people will hear you, no doubt about it.

Finally in this section, you can exercise your energy and ability to be heard by having some fun with language.

Try swearing, old style!

Shakespeare's plays are full of the most wonderful insults, in language that is not current but certainly very descriptive and powerful.

Try uttering Shakespearian insults as a vehicle for using your voice with energy and intention. This can work particularly well if you do it with a partner or in a group.

Just swear exceedingly loudly at each other in Shakespearian language, for example:

Thou Bawdy Beef-witted Barnacle!

Thou Beslubbering Clapper-Clawed Clotpole!

Pick three Shakespearian words at random from below to create a glorious, full-bodied insult! Take it in turns to outdo each other.

"Thou …
Bawdy Beef-witted Barnacle!
Beslubbering Boil-Brained Bugbear!
Craven Common-Kissing Canker-Blossom!
Dankish Doghearted Death-Token!
Fawning Fat-Kidneyed Foot-Licker!
Gleeking Gorbellied Gudgeon!
Lumpish Loggerheaded Lout!
Haggard Half-Faced Hugger-Mugger!
Impertinent Ill-Nurtured Idiot!
Puny Puking Maggot-Pie!
Mewling Milk-Livered Moldwarp!
Paunchy Pox-Marked Pignut!
Rank Toad-Spotted Scut!
Spongy Swag-Bellied Strumpet!
Weedy Unchin-Snouted Whey-Face!
Surly Onion-Eyed Measle!
Pribbling Hell-Hated Harpy!"

from *The Shakespeare Insult Kit*[9]

Now channel this level of energy into everything you say.

People will listen to you if you are utterly confident that you have something to say. Any uncertainty or hesitation will get in the way of being heard. Be confident that you do not need to shout or rush. You just need high energy and single-minded intention.

Then people will listen to your every word.

Chapter Nine

How can I sound more confident?

Life is too short to be little. Man is never so manly as when he feels deeply, acts boldly, and expresses himself with frankness and with fervour.

Benjamin Disraeli

You will find material throughout this book to help you increase your confidence as a speaker. In this chapter, we look particularly at specific easy techniques that will make a marked difference to your general feeling of confidence and in how you come across.

People often want to be able to speak with more authority, gravitas or maturity. These abilities all stem from confidence and you will learn these skills in this chapter too.

Well-balanced posture

We have talked before about posture and basic relaxation. Standing or sitting in a confident way instantly makes you look like someone to be reckoned with and makes you feel more confident inside. The balanced posture also gives your voice the best base for good sound. Remember to take a good breath and feel the air enter your whole body. As you breathe out, release your jaw and facial muscles, drop your elbows and every part of your body.

Your breath is always moving and a well-balanced posture is not static. Once you stick in a posture, you become rigid. As you stand, feel the constant small adjustment of your feet to balance, feel your head gently leading your body upwards towards the ceiling. Feel also your back broadening in width. It's a subtle sensation of expansion.

This language of lengthening and broadening is used in the Alexander Technique, much practised by singers, musicians and actors. F. M. Alexander, who developed the technique, was a Shakespearian actor who developed chronic laryngitis while working as a performer. Embarking on a journey of self-discovery to cure his voice, he worked out ways to lengthen the spine and free compression in the neck area, and further, restore the balance of the whole body. Following his advice, you can restore natural posture and through release of tension gain a new feeling of calm and confidence.

From a tall, relaxed place, imagine yourself speaking from your body rather than from your head. Feel relaxation spread through you and allow your whole body to be part of the action.

Strong emphasis

Confident speakers use strong emphasis to great effect. So it will be good news that increasing your emphasis is really easy. Emphasis is a feature more of some languages than others. When you listen to French or Italian, the sentences glide along smoothly, even when the speaker gets passionate or agitated. English speakers sound far more heavily emphatic. If an Italian speaker wants to stress a particular word, he lengthens the syllable. The assured English speaker lands on certain words with a heavy stress and sails easily over the others. The stressed words are always the most important words in terms of *content*. Confident speakers stress these particular words more strongly than unconfident speakers.

Try it out in the following lines:

This above **all**: to thine **own self** be **true,**
And it must **follow**, as the **night** the **day,**
Thou **canst** not **then** be **false** to **any** man.

or in a business example:

The **new strategy** has **important** implications in terms of **time** and **money.**

If when you practise you make a hand gesture with each emphasis it helps you to be conscious of the impact of the word and to create the strong effect. You don't need to keep the hand gesture as part of your style when you are not practising—unless you really want to!

Listen to commentators and interviewers in the media. If you copy the way they lay the stress on particular words you will probably be surprised by how strong the emphasis feels when you do it yourself. In listening, we are thoroughly used to the effect and probably don't notice it at all.

Stress and meaning

Stress is especially important for bringing out the sense of a sentence, as any change of stress affects the meaning, sometimes fundamentally:

"**I'm** not going"
(not me; maybe someone else, you, he or she)

"I'm **not** going"
(I refuse to go)

"I'm not **going**"
(It's not **going** I'm doing, it's coming back!)

Notice that negatives always need to be stressed to be correctly understood:

We **can't** under**stand** your reser**vat**ions about the **new plan-**ning **sys**tem.

If you don't stress *can't*, the listener tends to hear the word, *can*, just because of the lack of emphasis. It's a mistake that non-native speakers often make, sometimes with disastrous results!

Un-emphasised sounds

You hear the sounds /ɜ:/ (the vowel sound in "bird" and "heard") and /ə/ (the last vowel sound in "water" and "faster") quite naturally in English on unaccented words, and if we are a bit lazy in our speech every syllable turns into a version of these sounds. A flattened voice colours every vowel with an overlay of /ɜ:/ and /ə/ with a dreary effect. In order to transform our speaking voice for the better, we need to let some of the real vowel sounds come into their own.

However, it is quite usual in English for many of the un-emphasised sounds to be spoken with an "er" quality about them. Hear, for example, how many times these sounds naturally occur in the following sentence when we speak at normal speed:

The purpose of this oration is to communicate to the assembled circle the considerable importance and worth of manipulating the facial muscles as well as pronouncing the words.

Thə pɜ:rpəse əf thəs əratiən əs tə cəmmunicate tə thə əssembləd cɜ:rcle thə cənsidərəbl importənce ənd wɜ:rth əf mənipulating thə faciəl muscəls əs well əs prənouncəng thə wɜ:rds.

This is quite correct English pronunciation. To bring the sentence alive, we need to make clear vowels on the *emphasised* words, thus:

> Thə **pɜːrpəse** əf thəs əratiən əs tə **communəcate** tə thə əssembləd **cɜːrcle** thə **considərəble importənce** ənd **wɜːrth** əf **manipulatəng** thə **faciəl muscəls** əs well əs **prənouncəng** thə **wɜːrds**.

Now, read the sentence above firmly and loudly, even bringing the edge of one hand down into the palm of the other on each emphasised vowel to make the point stronger.

It sounds convincing doesn't it?

Vocal introductions

When you introduce yourself, your job and your company at the beginning of a speech, the sentence is content rich and therefore there are many words that need emphasising, for example:

"My name is **John Thom**pson. I'm **Chief** Engi**neer** of the **Lon**don **Power** and **En**ergy Company."

If you want to practise emphasis, introducing yourself is a great way to do it. Try it out in many different ways. When a sentence contains many important content words, you'll find you need to slow down considerably to fit in all the emphasised words without tripping over them.

Advertising slogans

A good place to find content rich sentences is in the world of advertising:

Persil washes whiter
Vroom, vroom
Melts in your mouth and not in your hand
Grab life by the horns
Finger lickin' good

Snap, Crackle, Pop!
Good to the last drop
Just do it

Practise announcing these with full rich emphasis.

Firm endings

Strong emphasis already makes a big difference. Now lower the voice pitch at the end of your sentences and you will sound even more confident. The ends of sentences are particularly important if you wish to sound authoritative. There are two pitfalls to avoid:

Avoid the rising inflection

As a general rule, a falling tone at the end of a sentence is used for statements and commands, and indicates completeness of thought. The rising tone indicates incompleteness and is used in all types of questions. If you use the rising tone at the end of a sentence that isn't a question, you will sound as if you are questioning your own statement and lacking confidence in what you are saying. The downward inflection sounds firm, as if you mean business. If you have a sentence with various sub-phrases, the strong downward inflection is usually reserved for the very end:

> There have been various problems, in India, in Pakistan, in many other parts of the world, but the main issue is right here at home, on our *door*step.

This gives you the strong low ending only on the syllable, *door*. The lowest emphasis is on the stressed syllable in the final word or short phrase. So if the sentence finishes with "a matter of principle", the "prin" of principle is the low emphasised syllable. In a sentence which concludes, "so let us all get used to it", "used" is the final low emphasised syllable.

There are certain accents that regularly have upward inflection at the end of a sentence, Australian being one, with programmes such as *Neighbours* a major world influence. People often call Australians friendly and rarely accuse them of being dictatorial: maybe the accent has a part to play in this impression.

Tony Blair as Prime Minister had a habit of ending sentences high, often with the tag, "you know". This questioning effect made him sound approachable but also made it more difficult for him to sound authoritative.

Avoid tailing off

If your voice tails off at the end of a sentence, either from lack of breath or from uncertainty, this will also give the impression that you lack confidence in what you are saying or that you don't care about it. Listen to George W. Bush for example, who never had a great reputation as a speaker. In a certain mode of delivery, he talks in short sentences and clips the end of each phrase, as if he's throwing the sentences away. It's hard to believe that he lays great store by an issue when he speaks in this way.

The remedy to this habit is to build your ability to breathe well so that you have sufficient breath to finish your sentences strongly, and to make sure that you end each sentence firmly on a low pitch.

The truth is that we respond more to intonation patterns than to the actual meaning of the words. Speak in an emphatic voice of authority and we believe you; say the same thing with a different intonation and we don't.

Practise ending your sentences firmly

Practise speaking sentences getting louder and firmer towards the end as an antidote to a tendency to tail off. Take any statement of your own or try the following:

"Many people find it hard to believe that the internet in so few years could change life for the general public as much as it **has**."

"The city of Phoenix in Arizona sits in the middle of a desert that for the past ten years has been suffering a punishing **drought**."

"The Commons select committee has just delivered a damning report on the major regeneration project that is the Thames **Gate**way."

Emphasise Shakespeare

We come back to Shakespeare's blank verse for speaking smooth phrases which end strongly. If you can speak these long dramatic phrases in full voice you will be equipped for all occasions. Try the following, and have fun with it, imagining that you are a great actor free of inhibition. Speak strongly and smoothly and build up the volume steadily in each phrase to the stressed syllable in bold. The final low-pitched stressed syllable is underlined.

To-morrow, and to-morrow, and to-**morrow**,

Creeps in this petty pace from day to **day**,
To the last syllable of recorded **time**;

And all our yesterdays have lighted **fools**
The way to dusty **death**.

Out, out, brief **candle**!
Life's but a walking **shadow**;

a poor **player**,
That struts and frets his hour upon the **stage**,
And then is heard no **more**:

it is a **tale**
Told by an idiot, full of sound and **fury**,
Signifying **nothing**.

(from *Macbeth*)

A deeper voice

As we have seen, a voice that resonates in the body, and particularly in the chest and solar plexus, sounds purposeful and trustworthy as well as being easy on the ear. If your voice is high pitched you might find that you are taken less seriously than someone with a lower voice. No wonder many public speakers have studied to acquire a lower voice.

Voices have fashions, and research at Flinders University in Australia has shown that women's voices have come down a few notes in pitch in the last fifty years. Listen to mid-twentieth century films and you will hear how much higher women's voices sounded at the time of the recordings. Celia Johnson in *Brief Encounter* would be a good example.

But just pushing your voice lower doesn't work very well. You will sound most confident and authoritative if you use your voice in the range that naturally fits your own vocal instrument. If you try to change your natural speaking voice by continually pushing it down to be more authoritative, you won't gain gravitas, and you might cause vocal damage.

First, check out your voice pitch

Remember that we cannot hear our own voices accurately from the inside, so your voice might not be as high as you think. Check with other people that you trust and ask them for feedback. Listen to a recording of your voice and be aware that recordings usually cut out some of the low resonance in your voice.

Optimum pitch

Your voice will sound most commanding if you stay within your own comfortable range.

Find your optimum low pitch with this exercise:

Find your comfortable pitch

In a ho-hum way, sing quietly a couple of lines of a simple song, like your national anthem or "Happy Birthday", in an easy, half-hummed

"Bom, bom-bom, bom" sort of voice. Then speak comfortably at that pitch.

Or this:

When someone speaks to you and you agree, say "Mmm" or "Umm" as a non-verbal encourager. When it's your turn to speak, come from the same pitch.

Breathe well

A high breath encourages an excitable, weak sounding voice, so learning to breathe using your diaphragm will help you produce a lower voice. This is the subject of Chapter 4. High breathing is often associated with making a slight gasp, so make sure that you breathe silently too. Be aware of the movements in your belly as you breathe gently and sense that your voice comes from that same place.

There are two main ways to lower your voice, using your pharynx and using increased chest and lower resonance.

Use more pharyngeal resonance

Margaret Thatcher, after coaching, became particularly adept at speaking in a deep pharyngeal voice and her low, rather breathy hushed tones became her trademark for media interviews. Lowering your pharynx makes a difference to the voice but as the adjustment is purely physical, and does not reflect inner thought and feeling, you can detect artificiality in the sound. It doesn't allow for much variety either, so gets rather monotonous after a while.

The effect is achieved by dropping the jaw and pressing it against the larynx. If you imagine that you are gargling marbles and speaking at the same time, you will get a good approximation.

One exercise used to strengthen the effect consists of a robust reci-tation of "Gha! Kha! Gha!" in the back of the throat. It's a useful exercise as a limbering-up and relaxation workout for the voice. However, if you use it doggedly to lower your pitch, it won't do your voice any good at all.

Use more chest resonance

If you want to sound confident and adult, your voice needs to resonate from your body as well as in your head. So the alternative to lowering your pharynx is to use more chest resonance as we learned in Chapter 6. This produces a clear, robust sound that has the ring of authority about it. It's a great way to improve your voice, and most speakers could benefit from developing it. Stand with a strong balanced physiology. As you pay attention to your chest and sense the sound coming from there, connect this sensation with the feeling of confident energy inside you. Then you will really feel and hear the difference.

Feel the difference between high voice and low voice

Place your hand on your chest and relax. Visualise your voice emanating from your chest or lower down instead of from your head, and then speak easily from that place.

Now speak again from your head. Hear the difference in voice quality.

Alternate the voices, and notice what you do differently to produce the body sounds.

Relax, accept

Your voice is affected by your state of mind. When you get fearful or try too hard, you tense up around the shoulders and neck and your voice tends to rise in pitch. Then, when you hear the higher voice, you may tighten up even more from anxiety, and set up a vicious circle. Breathe out, release the tension. Relax your shoulders and move your neck and jaw to release tension there. It will allow your voice to come out more naturally.

Accept that your voice today is your voice of today. You are OK. Your voice is OK. Just allow it to be.

Be at ease

These are some of the physical means to lower your voice, but remembering how closely your voice is connected with your psyche, you might want to examine psychological reasons for a high voice as well. One or more of the following might be an issue:

- A desire to sound feminine.
- A desire to please others or to come across as unthreatening or to get things right for others.
- Feeling stuck in a family role that has not been updated—of son or daughter for example.
- An unwillingness to show emotion, having trust only in matters intellectual.
- An unwillingness to express personal opinions.
- A lack of assertiveness.

Resolving such issues often allows access to a deeper voice without recourse to any further voice work. It will probably require you to work with a voice coach, but such issues can often be readily resolved through psychological methods such as NLP and related disciplines.

Confident articulate flow

You have more time than you think!

On those occasions when you are suddenly asked to speak without warning, time can play some strange tricks on you. A couple of seconds of silence can seem like a few minutes—or even an hour or two! You may feel a compulsion to plunge into words before you have even formulated an idea in your head.

But you don't have to …

… You have plenty of time …

… And will appear more confident if you use it.

So-o-o-o, take a good breath before you begin.

Breathe

Well, of course you breathe! But *how* do you breathe? A deep breath not only fills you with oxygen: it fills you with positive energy too. Breathing in will release your ability to think, and if you are called upon suddenly to speak, the first sentence can always be a preparatory remark such as, "Yes, thank you. I have a couple of things I'd like to say about that."

When you are anxious your breathing tends to be shallow. If you are very tense you almost seem to stop breathing altogether or you breathe high up in your chest, which is not an efficient way of taking in air.

In order to take in a really good breath, breathe out firmly first, feeling your whole body relax as you do so (relax the muscles, not collapse the bones!). Then welcome in the new air as it enters your body and feel its positive energy in every part of you.

A deep breath is like a new beginning. You leave behind the self of a moment ago and enter the self of now—the self that is ready to go. Taking a breath is a great way to move on if you lose the thread for a moment or get a sudden sense that things are not going well. Step into a new physical position away from the place in which you felt discomfort: literally take a step forward or to the side. Breathe in deeply, and move on with renewed energy.

You need breath to sound confident

Some people have a hesitant stuttering delivery, not due to any particular speech impediment, but because they take such inadequate breath that they must constantly stop and start, change tack, interject little asides, just to snatch little additional breaths.

If you want to sound confident, you need to be able to speak long phrases as well as short ones.

Try long energetic phrases

Practise speaking long phrases in a loud energetic way. It will build up your ability to breathe well. Here, Shakespeare comes in useful again. Once again, don the persona of a great actor—Sir Lawrence Olivier, Judy Dench, Ian McKellan, whoever is your favourite. Aim for a good robust voice, use a declaiming style and put lots of vital energy into your performance. Feel free to go "over the top".

Articulate flow

Try this quote to get you started—one breath for each paragraph and read in a strong measured pace. You might find the breaths long at first but with practice it gets easier.

Romans, countrymen, and lovers! Hear me for my cause, and be silent, that you may hear:
Believe me for mine honour, and have respect to mine honour, that you may believe:
Censure me in your wisdom, and awake your senses, that you may the better judge.
If there be any in this assembly, any dear friend of Caesar's, to him I say, that Brutus' love to Caesar was no less than his.
If then that friend demand why Brutus rose against Caesar, this is my answer:
—Not that I loved Caesar less, but that I loved Rome more.

(from *Julius Caesar*)

After Shakespeare, go to the great statesmen. Here is a quote from a war-time speech of Sir Winston Churchill:

I have, myself, full confidence that if all do their duty, if nothing is neglected, and if the best arrangements are made, as they are being made, we shall prove ourselves once again able to defend our Island home, to ride out the storm of war, and to outlive the menace of tyranny, if necessary for years.

Then you can try speaking from a presentation speech of your own or from other material such as a newspaper article, and put the same amount of energy into it.

Use your body as well as your head!

If you produce your voice mostly from your head and throat you can sound a bit childish or immature. The answer is to involve your body in the sound you make.

Relax your shoulders, neck and jaw to allow the breath to be felt right through your body.

Breathe low down. Allow your breath to flow; don't starve yourself of air.

Imagine that you are speaking from your body, not your vocal chords. Relax into your body and sense the sound coming from there.

Imagine yawning before you speak, to open yourself up.

Self-belief and sense of purpose

Come to the edge.
We might fall.
Come to the edge.
It's too high!
COME TO THE EDGE!
And they came
And he pushed
And they flew.

Christopher Logue, *Come to the Edge*
© Christopher Logue

Some people feel shaky when they speak in public, some go rigid and lifeless. In the former state your energy is needlessly dissipated; in the latter it becomes blocked. When you are nervous, the adrenaline you produce poisons your system and blocks your flow. So the answer is to use plenty of well-directed energy *before* the event, to rid your system of the adrenaline and allow yourself to feel alive and ready to go.

You may find some of the following helpful. Your choice of energiser will depend on your situation.

Physical energy preparation

Shortly before, if you can, go for a brisk walk to feel the energy flowing through your body.

Breathe out strongly and take in fresh air. Fill the bottom of your lungs and feel your whole body move in tune with the filling and emptying of air.

If the occasion allows, move your shoulders and stretch your body. If not, wriggle your toes inside your shoes and your fingers under the table or in your pockets!

Feel every cell in your body alive and tingling.

Smile to yourself inside, feel the smile in your body right across your chest, and enjoy the sensation of being fully alive and on your toes ready for anything. After the energetic activity, sense how much more alive you feel. Your audience will feel it too as you hit the ground running.

Bigger the occasion, bigger the energy

In a high pressure speaking situation you need more inner energy than you are normally aware of in your everyday way of being. Some speakers see this increase in energy as an important part of crossing a threshold from inner to outer you, from private to public, as you step forward to speak. If you have ever seen a great actor or performer from a position in the theatre wings, either on film or in real life, you will have witnessed the change that comes over him when he crosses from private into public mode. He breathes in and grows in stature before your eyes. Off-stage, he returns to normal size again. Some people comment on their surprise when they spot a celebrity in "ordinary mode" out in the street. "But she looked so small and ordinary when I saw her shopping in my supermarket!" they exclaim.

When you step up into high energy performing mode, it is not about pretending to be something you're not. It's like stepping into a larger you. Another way to think of it is to think of yourself at your most happy, most relaxed, most alive and step into *that* you.

That you can do anything.

> Think big, who ever heard of Alexander the Average?
>
> John O'Keefe

Change state – visualise

> It is the imagination that gives shape to the universe.
>
> Barry Lopez

What has visualisation got to do with voice? Quite a lot. Speaking starts with your imagination.

No, not to imagine disaster! Every time you think about drying up or tripping on the step you are helping to create a path to the fulfilment of such unwanted events. Imagine success instead. The master golfer Jack Nicklaus visualises the success of each shot before he makes it. He pictures the sequence in great detail, from the exact curve of the parabola of the ball to the exact place the ball will land.

The champion runner Carl Lewis considers visualisation a vital part of his performance preparation:

> Being spot on with your mental preparation is vitally important right from the first round. The night before each race I would go over the race in my mind and visualise what I had to do.[10]

Imagine success

You can do something similar for speaking occasions. Carl Lewis visualises himself crossing the finishing line first—again and again and again. So imagine success. Run through in your mind how you will walk on with confidence, acknowledge your audience with warm friendliness and say your first words with assurance and purpose. Visualise the warm response of your audience. Imagine the moment when you say something that has the audience hanging on your words. Hear yourself speak with confidence and energy. Hear the applause or positive response. Feel yourself relax as you see their interested faces. Sense the warmth of being with a group that is feeling a connection with you. Again and again, run over the desired scenario in your mind.

Not realistic? That doesn't matter. Just do it. And do it again. Each time it will get a bit more real, so that you get it "in the muscle" and your body knows automatically what to do. Then when you get to your live performance, the pattern is set. Whatever uncertainty your conscious mind throws up, your subconscious is already primed and knows what to do.

Your voice will reflect your state of mind. Change your state to a state of confidence through your imagination, and your voice will sound more confident.

You may find yourself still reluctant to visualise success. You can explain this away as fear of failure. But you need to ask yourself, do you *really* want to speak with assurance and confidence? What would you lose of *you* in being this way? How could you be confident *and* retain the core of who you are? Those are certainly questions that need addressing on your path to confidence and influence.

Act "as if"

> The essence of creativity is the ability to play.
>
> John Cleese

Sometimes, the willingness to pretend for a minute or two can produce results that months of dreary endeavour would not.

When I worked with Alice, a member of a legal firm, a few years ago, we spent several sessions without great progress. She was a quiet and highly intelligent person, and though she understood what she wanted to be able to do, there seemed to be no way that she could find to speak loudly or with any impact. I began to wonder if there were some people who could not be helped. We got to our fourth session and I asked her if there were any speakers she admired. She came up with an instant answer: "Well, the French directors, of course." I prodded further and she told me about two French directors who would come into their conferences with confidence and humour and gesticulate with energy. "Show me what they do," I requested. "But they're French!" she quickly responded, as if that closed the matter. "I understand that they are French," I said, "But even so, show me how they do it—just for curiosity."

With initial uncertainty, she walked to the centre of the room and began using her arms to gesticulate as she spoke. In a short space of time she forgot her embarrassment and began to speak in confident, robust tones with engaging humour.

When she came to a pause, I nodded. "Ah, so that's how they do it."

"Yes," she whispered in her normal tones, "Yes, that's what they do."

"It'd be great to be able to do that," I suggested.

"Yes," she agreed in her usual muted voice. "Yes, it really would."

It took quite another while for her to realise that she *had* done it, that it was in fact entirely possible for her to speak like that.

What is physically possible is not always mentally possible until one's beliefs catch up. When they did catch up for her, she realised that she could transform her voice in an instant, without further training or hard work or effort. It was possible, there and then— once she had sorted for herself the identity issue of what was "her" and what wasn't "her".

So, do something similar. Think of someone who possesses some of the characteristics you would like to have when you speak. The

113

person does not have to be a professional presenter—they could be a sports personality, a comedian, a friend who commands attention when a group of you meet, a historical figure ... anyone, from any walk of life, alive, dead or fictional. Think about what you admire in them. Is it their relaxed attitude, their humour, energy, way of connecting with you, the feeling that they care—all of these? When you have a good sense of what it is about them, imagine yourself *being* them and step into a rehearsal of your presentation *as* them—adopting their way of standing and moving, their facial expressions and tone of voice.

> Imagination is the beginning of creation. You imagine what you desire; you will what you imagine; and at last you create what you will.
>
> George Bernard Shaw

You might feel a bit self-conscious the first time, but repeat it, act "as if" this is something you can do effortlessly, and you will find that much of what they do easily becomes incorporated into your performance.

This is a great way to increase the impact of your voice. By "being" other people you can do all that you can imagine. The world's your limit. In time, whatever you "borrow" from any model will become yours, expanding your choices as a speaker.

The actor Jane Horrocks tells a story that supports this. In the film *Little Voice*, she plays the part of the lonely, timid Laura who spends her time obsessively listening to vintage recordings and impersonating great singers such as Edith Piaf, Shirley Bassey and Judy Garland. Jane Horrocks confesses that she did not even *have the notes* in her range to sing like these singers *until* she "became" them by impersonating them.

Giving yourself permission to speak

This last section sounds as if it should be the first. If you don't give yourself permission, you're not going to be able to speak at all. But many of us, most of us perhaps, speak without our own complete backing, and as a result speak in a voice which holds tension and fails to communicate freely.

Giving permission means letting go. When I gave my seven-year-old permission to walk to school on his own, I surrendered control. I was tempted not to: after seeing him off at the door, I thought of creeping behind him, hiding behind bushes and in gateways, to protect him and save him from danger. But I didn't. When I let him go, I let him go, and relied on my sense of trust.

This applies to the voice too. Giving yourself permission to speak means that you give yourself permission to say the wrong thing, to show unexpected emotion, to falter or pause. This is a very different thing from focusing on disaster: you just give yourself permission to be you, in your full humanity. When you do make mistakes, your lack of embarrassment will make them easy to deal with. Of course, the paradox is that if you give yourself permission to be human, the mistakes are actually much *less* likely to occur. So the only really sure way to a successful outcome is to let go of tight control.

It's like the tightrope walker who walks across the Niagara Falls. Tightrope walking requires balance and balance requires relaxation, a form of release. If the tightrope walker attempts consciously to control his safety, control creates stiffness, and stiffness spells disaster and inevitable death. So he *has* to let go of tightness to survive. That letting go is his salvation. It's an extreme message: relax or die!

Accept the moment. Whatever happens this moment happens this moment. And know for sure, that accepting the moment with trust is the way to the best of you, a strong confident voice and assured success.

Chapter Ten

How can I influence other people with my voice?

Voice and influence

It is not hard to affect others with your voice. Whenever it is heard by another person something happens. The other person may indeed hear it as just sound, even as irritating sound, or she may be profoundly affected by what you say and the way you say it. You will influence your listener *even if you don't mean to*.

So how can you exert influence over others in the way that you intend? Your voice is a major part of your communication and you can develop the changes to your voice that will allow you to exert influence.

There are just three essential factors:

- Your voice needs to create a positive impact, by being pleasant to listen to.
- You need to be in rapport with your listeners.
- Your voice needs to express your inner energy, including feeling and emotion.

Your voice needs to be pleasant to listen to

> You have all the characteristics of a popular politician: a horrible voice, bad breeding, and a vulgar manner.
>
> Aristophanes

Your voice will be pleasant to listen to if your body is relaxed and the voice is supported by breath with freedom to resonate. You also need some variation in the delivery. In other words, everything you have read so far in this book, which allows you to produce your voice well, also makes your voice pleasant to listen to.

How to create an impact

What actually has an impact on your listeners?

They need to be interested to follow you. So give them a trail to follow, not just in the sense of your words but in the way you say them.

When you travel by train, what gives interest to the journey? When you drive through varied scenery with plenty to look at, everyone perks up and looks out of the window. When the landscape stays the same for mile after boring mile, people begin to doze.

So you need to vary your landscape and this means:

Use the whole voice!

Look again at the vocal wheel to remind yourself of just how many ways you can vary your voice to create an impact:

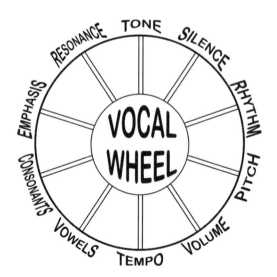

Resonance	– rich chest, warm heart, deep gut
Tone	– rough or smooth, silky or husky
Silence	– beautiful pauses
Rhythm	– dum-ti-dum, too-ti-ti-tooo, long phrases and short phrases
Pitch	– high and low
Volume	– loud or gentle, louder, softer
Tempo	– fast or measured, faster, slower
Vowels	– carriers of emotion, this is what it *feels* like
Consonants	– crisp articulation, clear understanding
Emphasis	– weight on words, hear <u>this</u>!

Achieving variation is not just a mechanical task. You need to know that you *can* vary your voice by practising all the different ways of speaking: fast and slow, loud and soft, rich and thin, high and low, light and emphatic. But then the sounds follow your thoughts. An important thought produces emphatic sound; an exciting thought produces high sound; a caring thought gentle sound; and so on. There are so many ways to vary your sound! No one ever need be bored again!

Just a note about self-consciousness: I know it can feel awkward to do something different with your voice; it can feel dangerous; it pushes the boundaries; it can even feel like invading other people too much. But remember that you are much *more* invasive with a dull voice. Just imagine what might be going on for your listener: "Who IS this person who dares to bore me in this way? Who does he think he IS?"

Rapport

Think us, not them and me

Your voice is affected by your state of mind, and your state of mind is affected by how you view your listeners. If you see them as potential adversaries or judges you will be on your guard from the word go. If, on the other hand, you see them as friends and supporters your attitude will be much more relaxed. "But they're *not* friends and supporters", you may say. How might they become so?

In *The Leader's Guide to Storytelling,* Stephen Denning tells the story of a classical singer whose accompanist is unavoidably late for a performance.[11] At the due time, the singer enters without her accompanist and in a spontaneous change of plan goes to sit on the edge of the stage where she starts to chat to the audience—about herself, her art, her life. By the time the accompanist arrives forty minutes later, singer and audience are the best of friends; and the rest of the recital has an intimate special quality that the performers have not experienced before. The different connection makes it *better* than before.

You don't need to believe your own inner conversations about, "This is an important audience", "There are experts there", "They don't want to hear this" and all the other things you may say to yourself. Your first job is to connect with the audience as human being to human beings. Begin speaking as if you were starting a dialogue and were expecting a response. People love you to relate to them. Queen Victoria complained of her stuffy Prime Minister, Gladstone: "He addresses me as though I were a public meeting."[12] Get the response instead: "He talks to us as if there were just the two of us in the room!"

Create a connection

> The play was a great success, but the audience was a disaster.
>
> Oscar Wilde

To be truly influential there needs to be a connection between you and your audience. It may be that you want your audience to be enthusiastic or you want to convince them, intrigue them, give them confidence. But if you just jump in with enthusiastic openings, convincing arguments or intriguing anecdotes when your audience has started off in a different mood, such as apathy or distrust, you are doomed to failure.

The solution is to begin at *their* starting point, not yours; and you discover what that is by stepping figuratively into their shoes and sensing the situation from their point of view. If the audience seems a bit hostile, start there; not hostile yourself, but with a similar energy, perhaps energised and prepared for opposition.

You might say something on the lines of, "I know that some of you may be asking yourselves if this session is going to be useful or not. If so, I'm keen to hear your experience, so that we can see what common ground exists ..." If the audience is apprehensive, start there: "You may be wondering why we are here today, and fearing a worst case scenario. I'd like to reassure you that things aren't *that* bad. In fact, I suspect that some of my proposals today might even come as a pleasant surprise ..."

This process is like gradually falling into step before you attempt to run together.

Empathise with your listeners

> The great gift of human beings is that we have the power of empathy.
>
> Meryl Streep

Connection starts with noticing your audience: with really seeing the people, listening to the sounds of their voices or the sound of their silence, and getting a "feel" of their mood and energy.

Watch someone who is empathetic. In a conversation with someone, when they sense a connection, they automatically adjust the way they communicate to fit easily with the other person. For example, if they meet a good friend, and she tells them she is feeling down, they will naturally speak to her in a lower voice at first, as they sympathise with how she is feeling and perhaps ask if she wants to talk about it. Some people spectacularly do the opposite in such circumstances, and brightly proclaim, "It's such a brilliant day today! Come on, snap out of it!" The response of most depressed people to such an approach is to feel misunderstood and slump a little deeper!

If the empathetic person meets a good friend who has just had a wonderful piece of good fortune, such as winning a million pounds, she naturally increases her internal energy to share enthusiastically in their excitement. She knows that to mutter in a jokey, grumpy voice, "Some people have all the luck", won't really be seen as humorous and will break the connection.

So, rapport is sharing the other person's way of experiencing the world. In practical terms, it shows in your sharing the physical aspects of their being in their world, through energy, breathing, body language and the voice. Many people adjust their voice entirely naturally when they speak with another person. Others will follow your vocal lead once you have established an empathetic connection with them.

If you metaphorically "step into the other person's shoes" you will adjust naturally. On occasions when it doesn't come naturally, you can deliberately accommodate your voice to fit the other person's, matching their tone, vocal pitch, speed, cadence, volume and rhythm.

Mostly it takes very little, maybe just a slight slowing down if you naturally speak much faster than the other person or a slightly louder or quieter tone to match their tone. When you do this, the other person feels the harmony between you and relaxes. At this point there opens up the possibility of mutual influence.

Influence through feeling

I've learned that people will forget what you said, people will forget what you did, but people will never forget how you made them feel.

Maya Angelou

Once you have created a connection with the other person or audience, and only then, they will be influenced by your state of mind. So get in a real state!

If you want them to get enthusiastic, be enthusiastic. If you want to inspire passion, be passionate. Catch the emotion yourself. An audience is influenced as much by your state of mind as by the content of what you have to say, so don't hold back. You can communicate emotion successfully only by entering into the emotion yourself. If you talk about excitement in a flat voice, your audience will fail to pick it up. If something matters to you, show that it matters; if something excites you, get excited, and your delivery will be a great success. Your voice needs to express your inner energy, including feeling and emotion.

When Hillary Clinton was fighting for the Democratic nomination in the United States, the spirit she showed most often was that of the fighter. But there was one occasion in an interview where she struggled with her emotions and came very close to tears as she murmured, "I just don't want to see us fall backwards." At that point, the nation caught hold of her passion and in the following days her ratings enjoyed a sudden improvement. What may have seemed to her like a moment of weakness was recognised as a moment of genuine feeling by the public, and they warmed to her.

You will assert a much stronger influence if you are *associated* into the particular state of mind you wish to convey. In other words, you need to be able to *feel* the feeling or emotion in real time. How influential can you allow yourself to be? The answer is, to the extent that you allow yourself to be you. Step into a larger you, you at your best and most confident. As you allow yourself to be real, authentic and happy in your skin, so will you exert a strong influence on others.

Sound charismatic

People who are able to exert a strong influence are sometimes called charismatic, a word that stems from the Greek *charis* meaning "grace".

123

There is a grace in the way some people walk and there is a grace in the way some people talk. The voice sounds charismatic when there is a match between the tone of voice and the sentiment being expressed, where there is no awkwardness between the idea, emotion or thought and how it is expressed through sound. The resonance of the voice is in keeping with what is being expressed.

A speaker who is charismatic is all of a piece, "connected inside", when he is communicating with people. "Happy in his own skin" would be another description. A charismatic speaker also knows how to connect with the audience so that those listening feel at one with him. This is achieved when the speaker is free of self-consciousness and able to communicate authentically as himself. Again, being "happy in your own skin" is the key.

People who are charismatic have a deep internal energy, a "life force" which reveals itself whenever they speak. You will have the greatest impact on others when you possess vibrant energy. This does not mean that you have to be over-forceful or manic; the inner energy is just as evident in a peaceful demeanour and a quiet voice as in a thunderous way of expressing yourself.

Be yourself

> I have often thought that the best way to define a man's character would be to seek out the particular mental or moral attitude in which, when it came upon him, he felt himself most deeply and intensively active and alive. At such moments, there is a voice inside which speaks and says, "This is the real me."
>
> William James

Did an adult ever say, "Just be yourself", as an encouragement when you faced some challenge as a child? And if they did, did you ever wonder, "What on earth is that supposed to mean?"

How exactly can you be yourself? Most people adopt roles in their lives and many feel the sense of "putting on the uniform" as they step into the part of leader, manager, expert and so on. The uniform or status can feel as if it lends you a power that you don't have as "just you".

Yet the wonderful paradox is that you are most powerful when you reveal the truth of who you are, for people then have a real person to relate to. You might feel safer if you hide behind formality or rigid role play but you won't be communicating as directly and the audience won't feel the same connection.

> Always be a first-rate version of yourself, instead of a second-rate version of somebody else.
>
> Judy Garland

Self-consciousness is the great enemy of good presenting, taking you away from *being* yourself to consciousness *of* yourself. One major element of self-consciousness is your insistence that everything *has* to be a certain way for you to be successful. You will recognise this in yourself as the inner voice of "musts" and "shoulds": "This has *got* to be good because my most important client is in the audience", "I *must* try not to stutter", "I *can't* be seen to blush", "I *ought* to know more than I do", "I *should* be able to communicate this without having to read it".

The psychologist, Carl Rogers, when called upon as he often was to speak in public, found it a daunting experience. Before going on stage, he would remind himself, "I am enough." And he always was.

It is quite true. You *are* enough. Just as you are. Now. At this moment.

You are enough.

Influence and trance

Influence usually works below the level of people's conscious awareness. This is the case when you send people into trance either informally or through a formal hypnotic induction.

Hypnotic induction works through "going with" the client's responses as you lead them. So when you notice the client relax her shoulders for instance, you may say, "And as you feel the softness in your shoulders, you are able to breathe even more easily ..."

This creates rapport between you but you are using your voice to create rapport not with their tone of voice as in a conversation but with their silence.

The resonance that connects best with silence is the voice of the gut that gently resonates from low in your body throughout your whole body. As we have seen above, this voice connects with our deep instinct and innermost being. In contrast to the voice of the head that is often quick and bright in its enthusiasm and excitement, the voice of the gut is soft and slow, with pauses, allowing one sound to permeate your whole being before you move to the next.

As you speak, you feel your connection with the client's body language and general energy, and translate that feeling into sound. It requires good breath support to be able to do this, both to place weight on particular words and to make the phrases long and slow enough to be really effective in leading the client deep into themselves.

The hypnotic skill of influence clearly rests on skilful use of imagery and language that can enter the client's mind without jarring, and then gently lead them to a better place internally. The tone of voice is the vehicle that allows this to happen, and the deeper you go into the psyche, the lower, quieter and slower the voice becomes.

When this is done well, the listener has the sensation that the voice he is hearing and feeling vibrating within actually *arises* from within himself. Any positive thoughts expressed by you are then heard as an auto-suggestion rather than something imposed from the outside.

Similarly, you can entrance your listeners informally during a presentation when you wish to influence them deeply at some point. You increase your attention on what you have to say, you lower and quieten your voice and decrease your pace, and your listeners follow you to a deeper, more inward place. You will be aware of the quality of their silence as they attend to you in semi-trance.

When you want to bring your listeners or client out of trance, you have only to change your voice gradually to effect the change. You begin to use a brighter tone, to increase the volume slightly and to speak a little faster, and they will follow you outward back into the everyday again.

Be in the now

> At the still point of the turning world there the dance is. And without the point, that still point, there would be no dance. And there is only the dance.
>
> T. S. Eliot, "Burnt Norton", *Four Quartets*

You hear about speakers having "presence". You may have felt a sense of presence when you listen to certain speakers. I used to think that this wonderful magical quality of presence was something too mysterious to define or capture. But I gradually discovered that presence is in fact very simple. You just have to *be present*, that is, aware in the moment. Being present means that you are literally focused on the here and how. You are not thinking about past disasters or future fears of failure or judgement, nor are you remembering your past successes and looking forward to future triumph. You are just in the moment, second by second by second.

Sometimes even the best presenters say something that was ill-advised or a mistake and get pushed off balance. The moment you begin to worry or feel wrong-footed you are no longer in the present. Worry takes you back to the mistake and forward to anxiety about the consequences. You have left the present. And your audience becomes aware at some level of your absence. Take a good breath and create a new beginning. Become present again. Every second is a new present.

In the present you will be aware of everything in your visual field through 180 degrees from left to right. Your peripheral (sideways) vision is especially aware of movement and picks up a clear sense of what is happening at the present moment. Through this vision you will capture the essential mood of the people in your audience, how focused, how engaged, how restless they are.

What happens to your voice when you are in the now? Simply a miracle. Your voice settles down and does what it has to do. All the worries about tightness, or high pitch, or swallowing, or breathi-

127

ness disappear. Your voice expresses the moment. And other people catch the moment.

> At the centre of your being you have the answer; you know who you are and you know what you want.
>
> Lao-Tzu

Part Four

The Heart of the Matter

Chapter Eleven

Inspiration

One day last year I heard Sir Bob Geldof speak at a business conference. He didn't follow any traditional public speaking conventions as they are generally understood. He paced up and down doggedly avoiding the eyes of his audience, he talked quietly as if for his own benefit alone and only stopped to look at us for the first time after several minutes.

Yet as a speaker he was riveting, and judging by the comments afterwards, influenced his audience deeply. How so? As we seek to answer that question, we find that there is more to successful public speaking than we might suppose. The basic elements of good speech will help you to come across clearer and stronger. But there is much more to it than that, as you realise when you witness charisma in action. When an influential communicator speaks, it is no longer just words: you sense the person. *Through* the words you feel the power of the individual and what he has to offer the world. The sense you have of him inspires and energises you.

How does it work? How does someone inspire others?

In this chapter we explore what lies within the speaker beyond skill and technical ability. We examine charisma; and that brings us back to the breath.

Physical breathing and intentional breathing

We already know that breath initiates the voice and is the source of its energy. Well, of course it is! It's the life of everything: we breathe and live, we expire and die. We associate breath with more than just being alive: it is the thread that connects our physical, mental, emotional and spiritual systems. The Book of Genesis tells us, "the Lord God formed man of the dust of the ground, and breathed into his nostrils the breath of life; and man became a living soul."

In the traditional Maori "hongi" greeting, two people share and intermingle the breath of life or "ha" when they rub noses. There are substantiated accounts of wild horses becoming calm when someone breathes gently into their nostrils.

Let's look a little closer at what we actually do when we breathe. We breathe before we do anything purposeful, and it's especially obvious before physical action. Try striking a nail with a hammer or jumping in the air without taking a breath first—you'll find it difficult to do. The harder you want to hit the nail or the higher you want to jump, the more you will fill yourself with air first.

Now, when we communicate we breathe beforehand as with most actions, but the very act of speaking *consists* of moving breath. Because the sound we make is actually made up of vibrating air the breath has a particularly intimate connection with the physical act of producing our voice.

It's a psychological act too. Breathing is not just the machine that moves air to make the vocal cords vibrate. It is the life and intention behind the desire to speak, and in a very direct way, how you take in breath determines how you will sound.

Most sudden energetic impulses in us will produce breath and sound. If a car just misses you as you begin to step off the pavement, you gasp and exclaim, "Whew!" When you are frightened by a sudden movement, you may give a little shriek, "Oh!" If someone suddenly barges into your body you respond with, "Hey!" When the big dipper train goes over the curve and suddenly plunges, you cry, "Wheee!" Each of these auto-responses is preceded by an intake of breath that matches the response.

Your breath connects to the felt sense within you, and importantly, it connects to your *intention*. When you have the impulse to speak your intention determines *how* you breathe. A particular intention produces one kind of breath; another intention produces a different breath. In this chapter we will see just how this intention, the impulse to speak, connects with the breath to create influential communication.

Intention is the key. It provides the sense of purpose that leads to action, and it vibrates with desire. Desire's energy comes from a spark within, which is a *felt* sense. Desire is essential to the words and actions of every human being. The founder of modern coaching, Tim Gallwey, calls it "the source and fuel of everything". "Desire", he says "is vital to the navigation of the human being. It pulses when you are near … It is feeling the feeling and then doing."[13]

Desire plays a large part in all successful natural learning. Think, for example, how a child learns to walk. Walking is a complex process: if you were to write the instruction manual it would probably run to several pages. But what happens in practice? The toddler stands on her feet a few paces away from her carer. She sees the smiling encouraging face, the open arms, and feels desire. She launches herself with the intention to reach the smiling face and covers the distance successfully to arrive at the place where she wants to be. If she falls, she doesn't lose the desire; she scrambles to her feet again and launches herself towards the smiling face once more.

Speaking is more complicated than walking. The larynx alone has more nerves than the hand or foot. The method of learning however is the same. You feel a desire (to communicate) and you launch (into sound) with purpose and intent.

Energy and desire

> Energy is eternal delight.
>
> William Blake

Where do we experience desire? We can *think* about what we want and *reason* about what we want in the head, but desire is *felt* in the body, in the heart or in the gut, and provides the vital energy that turns thought waves into sound waves.

The description of "inner intelligence" by the thirteenth century Sufi poet, Rumi, comes close to describing this sensation in the body:

> There is another kind of tablet, one
> already completed and preserved inside you.

> A spring overflowing its springbox. A freshness
> in the centre of the chest. This other intelligence
> does not turn yellow or stagnate. It's fluid,
> and it doesn't move from outside to inside
> through the conduits of plumbing-learning …
> This second knowing is a fountainhead
> from within you, moving out.

Your voice emerges from your need to communicate, and your need to communicate arises from an energy which is experienced as an emotion, a state of mind. Even when I ask you to pass me the salt across the table, that small flicker of wanting my food to taste more interesting is the desire which precipitates the intention of asking for the salt. This energy is present in every communication. You feel the impulse to express joy, enthusiasm, determination, calm, confidence, trust, anger, warmth, gentleness, pity, fear or intimacy. Desire or intention initiates the breath, and most importantly, each desire or intention will set in motion a *different kind of breath*.

Different breaths for different thoughts

If you are delighted to see someone you feel the delight in your body, and that emotion causes your breath to react in a lively manner which in turn makes the vocal cords vibrate with vitality and the resonators in your body come into play freely. The process is infinitely varied and the resulting tone is lively and expressive with constantly modulating tones.

If you are genuinely surprised your intake of breath comes suddenly, and you really feel your diaphragm come into play, lowering and making the belly distend. If you go *immediately* from that feeling of surprise into words, the sounds are likely to be animated and bright or sharp—depending on the nature of the surprise!

If you are determined to voice something that matters to you that feeling of determination may cause a slow, firm breath, and the sound which emerges will resonate firmly in your chest. The firm intention and breath create the strong sound and steady pace that follows.

If you are excited, and want to share this with someone, you will probably take a short energetic breath and the resulting sound will be bubbly, full of energy and quite high pitched.

If you are exasperated and willing for another person to know what you are feeling, your breath is likely to be quick and full, and the sound you make will also be full of air.

Every time you breathe to speak you fill your lungs with air to set your vocal cords in vibration. But the muscles you use to cause air to enter your lungs, and how you use those muscles, will depend on the urgency and strength of your communication, the nature of the emotion, how long the sentence and so on. It will also depend on the tension in your body at that particular time. And beyond the use of your muscles, every cell in your body will play a part, and a different part each time, in this transformation of thought and feeling into sound.

Breathing with intention

Discover what different kinds of breath result from different intentions. Try this out for yourself, with a partner if possible.

Imagine that someone treads on your foot: if you can work with a partner get them to bang on the ground as if it is happening and then react immediately. What kind of breath do you take to exclaim, "Ouch!"? I expect it will be quick and full.

Or say something to each other which is a welcome surprise. Your partner offers you £10,000 which is entirely unexpected: how do you respond?

Ask each other different kinds of questions, or ask yourself the questions, and see how your breath changes for different answers when you go with the instinctive response. Use questions or comments that will provoke a strong response; here are a few suggestions to start you off, but the questions need to be appropriate to you:

Will you come into work in your holiday period?
Do you think that war is the only answer in the Middle East?
Do you like fried brains?

What is your idea of the dream holiday?
Your work is below standard, isn't it?
Can I borrow your car again this week?
You have just won the lottery!

Notice that the sounds of the response will link to the intention only if you are willing for the other person to hear your real intention. My excited comment will only sound excited if I allow this inner feeling or intention to be shared. Likewise with exasperation: if I'm willing for the other person to know my true intention, the voice will reveal the inner feeling in the sound.

If I'm not willing for this to be known, I will not allow intention/ breath to flow directly into sound, and the link between sound and meaning will be lost, *even if I say the same words I was intending to say.* We will come back to this, for it is a crucial element in how successful we can be in influencing others.

Inspiration

> Inspiration and genius—one and the same.
>
> Victor Hugo

Our purpose each time we speak is different, and thus the in-breath is also different. Our purpose creates an energy which is expressed *in the action of breathing in*, or "in-spiration" (from the Latin *inspirare*—in + spirare—to breathe). What is inspiration but that desire, the spirit moving into action? Without this desire, the voice has no inner life.

Inspiration refers both to the act of breathing in and to the act of creating a thought. Breathing in is both a physical activity and a mental/emotional expression: these mind and body functions go together. The word refers to the physiological process of preparing to speak or act; that is, the drawing of air into the lungs, and also to the divine influence or stimulus to do creative work.

The singer and voice teacher, Kristin Linklater, describes the connection between intention and sound:

> The natural voice is transparent—revealing, not describing,
> inner impulses of emotion and thought, directly and
> spontaneously. The person is heard, not the person's voice.[14]

Her last eight words say it all. When your breath leads straight from intention into sound, people hear *you*, not just the sound of the words. They *get you*, directly.

In our physical lives we go from breath straight into action all the time. I mentioned hitting a nail or jumping earlier. Whenever you kick a ball, dive into a swimming pool or take a swing with a tennis racquet, you breathe as you prepare for action, and go straight into carrying out the action. If you take a giant step forward from a standing position, you quite naturally breathe in as you launch into the step. And then you take the step. In fact, you have no choice at this point as you step beyond your point of balance and gravity takes over to complete the movement.

In speaking, gravity does not take over, so you have the choice to interrupt the movement in the middle at the top of the breath. This is one of the principal ways in which people block their natural voice. So, as an exercise to prevent such interruption, try combining physical movement with your voice, letting the voice mirror the physical pattern.

Move and speak!

With a good breath take a giant step forward, bending your knees naturally as you land on the front foot.

Now repeat, adding a robust sound as you land: "Haa!" Hear how freely the voice comes out.

After trying that a couple of times, think of some real issues in your life that you would like to respond to or express. For example, think of something you passionately want to say yes to, and step forward energetically with that thought, landing on the sound, "Yes!" And again, even louder, "YES!" Then find something you firmly, strongly say "no" to, and step forward energetically with that thought, landing on a robust, "No!" And again "NO!" Now try with other words to which you respond strongly. What would they be—"Stop!" "Go!"

"Wow!"? Each time, have a specific idea in your mind which lends energy to the action and sound.

Now you can practise that sensation of going straight from breath into sound with the voice on its own. The in-breath can emerge out of many different kinds of energetic impulse. Let's take an example where you breathe in with a quiet energy.

The scented breath

Imagine a beautiful smell. What would that be for you—a rose, honeysuckle, the smell of a log fire in winter, the scent of pine, warm bread in the oven? Breathe in through your nose, creating the smell in your mind and breathing it in. Even as you are still breathing in, say something out loud in response to the smell. The words do not matter: the expression of your pleasure does.

For example, I breathe in, smelling a favourite perfume, wild honey-suckle, and even as I do so, the words slip out, "Oh, what a beautiful smell."

If your words arise entirely from your pleasure in the smell you will find that your voice is soft edged and seems to come from a place quite low inside you. It will also have a resonance that is musical to the ear.

Of course, once you begin to utter words you are not strictly still breathing in, but the inner sensation is of the act of breathing in flowing straight into speech without any hiatus between: breath just transforms into sound.

If you find it difficult to flow from the in-breath straight into words, try this instead: breathe in with the same imaginative thoughts in your mind as before, begin to sigh out with the pleasure of your favourite smell, and then while you are releasing the air, slip from out-breath into speech, with an appreciative comment as before.

You can try this exercise with different feelings such as excitement, anger, determination or boredom. For example, access the feeling of excitement and the desire to express it, and then say whatever you say. You need to access the relevant feeling authentically. One way to do this is to remember vividly a time when you felt in that particular way. Go back to that occasion, be right there, right in it, feeling what you felt at the time, and then take that feeling into the exercise.

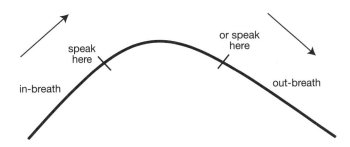

You might be surprised at the extent to which your voice changes with your different internal processes when you just allow the voice to emerge naturally from the feeling/intent expressed in the breath.

Now the thought might occur that "allowing" your voice to come out as it wants in this way is not totally practical, for there are going to be many times when you don't want to speak uncensored. In the American film, *Liar Liar*, the protagonist finds himself blurting out aloud whatever is in his head for a whole day.[15] It is pure comedy for us but a day of agonising embarrassment for him. You certainly would not choose to be so transparent in real life. You may have been like that when you were three years old but you soon learned that to blurt out spontaneously whatever you were thinking or feeling was not the way to survive in the world!

Don't worry! You still have time to think before you speak but that time is *before* you breathe, not between breath and utterance. If you think before breath you can proceed straight from breath into sound. So the old advice, "Think before you speak" becomes more accurately, "Think before you breathe!"

Adding "expression"

Connecting intention to its expression in sound is totally different from adding expression to what you say. Often, when someone has a speech to deliver, a script is produced and the speaker learns how to read it "expressively". Sometimes, a speaker even asks for "stage directions" to be added to the script of a professional speech, thus:

> Ladies (high voice) and gentlemen (low voice), we are <u>very</u> (high voice, stressed) happy to welcome MARY SMITH (heavy emphasis, highest pitch) to our development team (lower tone, smile at audience).

The comedian Rory Bremner used to present a sketch of Tony Blair, where he recited a whole speech, including the instructions. It was a neat way to poke fun at his ability to act in front of an audience.

When so many political speeches are written in full and then read by busy politicians with added expression, we get very used to speeches delivered with expression stuck on. No wonder we feel we're always getting the same old thing!

Why is it that this method is not entirely successful as a means of convincing an audience? It's because the link between intention and sound has been lost. Listen for yourself. You can usually hear quite clearly on the radio whether the speaker is reading out a script or speaking completely spontaneously or freely from headline notes. When she is reading with expression pasted on the stresses and variations in pitch are heavy-handed and all the sparkle and subtlety of variation is lost—apart from rare cases where the speaker has learned to recreate a written script so that it sounds new.

Listen with half an ear to a news broadcast. You will find that the shape and emphasis of sentences is fixed and predictable. What appears on the surface to be a varied and energetic delivery is in fact often a hackneyed remake of the same old highs and lows, emphases and pauses. No wonder the twentieth century term, "sound bite", has become associated with the superficial and the glib. The speech writer invents the sound bite and the speaker "adds" the expression on top. Thought is separated from sound and therefore cut off from its life blood.

There are lots of entertaining examples of speeches with added expression in public life. I was on an aircraft recently when the leader of the cabin crew gave an announcement. Her attempts at expression created odd emphases that turned the whole utterance into nonsense:

> Ladies AND gentlemen, we would like TO welcome you on board this Boeing 747 bound FOR Nice. There WILL now be a short safety demonstration and we would ask you TO pay attention—thank you.

This stock way of adding expression often makes it difficult to tell whether the news is good or bad. Back in the airport there were two announcements, one after another, in precisely the same warm, soft tone with similar emphasis. What follows is a slightly creative version:

> We WOULD like to ask passengers flying to Nice ON flight BA 2764 to proceed TO the check-in area—thank you.

> We WOULD like to inform passengers that all bags left unattended WILL be blown up BY our security staff—thank you.

Negatives of disconnecting from the breath

At any time during the sequence of breathing and speaking we have the opportunity to interrupt and control the natural process of thought and feeling turning into sound. As soon as we step in to control the natural impulses, the intuitive process of intention becoming sound is interrupted. This happens when we feel angry but speak without anger, or feel upset and speak as though we are unconcerned or, as in some media communications, feel bored but speak as if we are energised.

Mismatch

Now, this ability to check ourselves serves a useful purpose; it is indeed part of the process of growing up and is sometimes described in ways which the world would applaud, such as "tact", "discretion" or "diplomacy". However, we can be so conditioned to this process of checking ourselves that we speak habitually in a voice that does not connect at all to what is going on inside us.

One of our neighbours never has a harsh word to say about anything or anyone. She talks about how lucky she is compared to others less fortunate, how she counts her small blessings and enjoys watching people be happy. But listening to her is a bit like hearing a man burning at the stake saying how content he is not to be drowning. Listening to this woman is to hear chirpy, cheerful sounds on the surface, and to enter an unspoken, unheard world of sadness and disappointment. This is not apparent if you listen just to her words. But if you tune in to tone and rhythm, the sound behind the sense, and in particular pay attention to the onset of the sound, the underlying message is clear.

I have been interviewed on local radio programmes from time to time, often at an unsociable hour of the morning. One programme anchor has been communicating with his loyal audience for many years, listening to their stories, rejoicing in their successes, fielding their whinges and complaints. He has done it professionally and competently, and now is ready to move on. The early mornings have taken their toll; the micro-concerns of listeners no longer fascinate him. In the interludes of music and other events between his slots, I watch him yawn and stretch. He raises a sympathetic eyebrow to me at a particularly inane comment and shakes his head at the tedium of a particular article. He makes the odd exasperated comment in the musical interludes. Then, suddenly, he is back on the air, and his voice kicks in, enthusiastic, full of beans, joking: sound bites, laughter. Again, music cuts in, and his whole face switches off. He is adopting vocal expression, not communication, and there is a difference.

There's a difference in the sound. With "expression" there are regular rhythm and pitch patterns; there's less variation in pace, less subtlety in the sounds. There is a difference in his effect on us too: he can energise but not move us. And you can spot the difference in the breathing. When you speak in a natural lively way, the breathing is an integral part of the process, not something you do first and then inhibit. It's that life in the breath turned into sound that connects in a direct way with the listener. If you take a breath and then hold back what you are about to say for a micro-second to veto feeling before giving utterance, your speech is disconnected from your life and intention.

This micro-second of disconnection is often audible as a slight check or even glottal stop at the beginning of each sentence. A colleague asks someone if he has had a good holiday. The direct connected response comes straight away with enthusiastic breath and warm sound: "Oh yes, we had a great time, thanks!" The disconnected response clicks in after a micro-pause and sounds dry, "Uh, yes, thanks, yes, lovely time." That "uh" sound can be very subtle, but with some people it pounds against the vocal cords every time they open their mouth, which tires the voice. Or it closes down throat and mouth and initiates a reduced, constricted sound.

So there is a physical downside to holding back: if you are not speaking with free breath, you are likely to compensate by over-using your throat and mouth muscles. Alternatively, you drive the sound up into the face mask or nose where it sounds hard and monotonous. Or you make so much effort that the vocal cords touch each other and gradually lose the elasticity that makes the sound vibrant. In the worst cases, the cords grow nodules and become damaged.

Disconnected voice

Lack of connection between breath and voice is not always so obvious. There is a way of monitoring your sound which produces a voice that is well-modulated but still disconnected. When I met Sandy, the first thing I noticed was his richly resonant voice that impressed people with its confidence and ease. But there was a regularity about it that made what at first sounded expressive begin to pall. At one point he told me about an exciting piece of good fortune that had come his way: he had been selected to speak in a prestigious slot at a large national conference. "That's fantastic!" I exclaimed, my voice rising enthusiastically. "Yes, it's really exciting," he agreed, and his voice remained beautifully modulated and lugubrious. It was like listening to Eeyore in *Winnie the Pooh*.

The more I listened to Sandy, the more I became aware of the lack of light and shade in his voice. He only did rich and resonant. He spoke in frustration: rich and resonant. He felt anxious: rich and resonant. He was pleased to see you: rich and resonant. His voice did not express his thoughts at all: rather, it disguised them. It was manufactured, like an actor's mask. In fact, this rich, resonant sound is the voice that certain actors adopt, and whilst we can stand back and admire the resonant tones, the delivery always sounds artificial. You hear "the actor". You always feel you are being talked "at" rather than "to".

Many of us live in the world in an assumed identity or role, much like an actor. We *take on* a personality for a particular job or role. The role may become so familiar that we don't even remember that it is a role, until sometimes life's circumstances take it away from us. But our voice reveals the masquerade.

Sandy always took that fraction of a second between breathing in and speaking to lower his larynx and "put his voice on". I think if I had jumped on Sandy's foot, he would still have taken that microsecond before responding in his habitual voice, "Er, actually, that was quite painful, er, I'd rather you didn't do that again": rich and resonant!

Such a voice, though pleasant to listen to at first, is ultimately monotonous as it lacks variation and fails to reveal the real person behind the voice. One voice tone serves for all emotional purposes instead of tones that are infinitely varied and lively. Though congenial, the sound does not express what is going on and therefore doesn't really make a connection with others. The listener is deceived—and often the speaker is deceived as well! So, the voice, as well as being a vehicle to express our thoughts and feelings, can also be a front, to prevent people discovering what is going on inside.

What are the differences and how can we detect them?

How can you tell that the voice is manufactured? Mostly by the fact that the voice lacks light and shade. Whether the person is happy, sad, upset or determined, the voice sounds much the same. Kim Philby's plummy tone when he deceived his interrogators was such a voice. His tone gave nothing away.

Connecting and disconnecting

A voice that never changes is always a sure sign of a disconnected voice. You can test the effects for yourself. Make the following statements all in one tone of voice, keeping the same pitch level.

"That was unforgivable. How dare you!"
"It was the most beautiful day of my life"
"Mine's a cheese and chutney please"

Now repeat them, thinking about what you are saying and allowing the energy of each statement to come into your voice.

"That was unfor**giv**able. How **dare** you!"
"It was the most **beau**tiful day of my **life**"
"Mine's a **cheese** and **chut**ney please"

Do you notice how your voice varies in pace and emphasis, and how the accented syllables have a different pitch? Each statement creates a totally different impact.

In our times, the "sound bite" voice is all-pervasive. Our ears are thoroughly attuned to hearing voices that do not connect with genuine impulses. This makes it harder for us to detect micro-differences and we need to train ourselves to become more sensitive to sounds.

Where does the artificial voice come from? At some time in his life, someone who speaks like this separated emotion from expression. He made the decision (out of conscious awareness probably) not to reveal everything that was going on inside—in other words to put up a mask to hide emotions that perhaps didn't seem acceptable.

The effort caused tension—often in the shoulders, the neck and the jaw. This tightness cuts you off from expressing yourself fully. If you close your throat or grip your jaw, you are cutting your thinking brain off from your feelings, emotions and natural impulses. You will never get an instinctive response from someone who speaks with such tension—there is always an infinitesimal pause before they react.

If you hold yourself tightly inside, swallow what needs to be said, care too much about what others think and suppress your real nature, you will not find your truly inspirational voice. If you adopt a fake voice or an obsequious voice, in time you forget what your own voice is and, losing your voice, you lose yourself.

The free voice

The voice that is truly expressive is free of chronic body tension. If your voice is free, the sound resonates in all parts of your body, communicating every nuance of what you have to say. Hundreds of bones and muscles in your body are involved in conveying your meaning through resonance. As you become excited, your voice goes up in pitch for a moment; as you sound determined, the voice resonance increases in your chest; as you express care or concern, your voice comes more from your heart. The voice does this automatically, constantly varying, reflecting spontaneously the nuances of your communication in different proportions of resonance from different parts of your body.

One of the finest voice coaches of our age, Cecily Berry, who worked for many years as the voice director of the Royal Shakespeare Company, and taught many of our greatest actors, said: "Speaking is part of a whole: an expression of inner life."

How glorious it is to listen to a voice that is communicating from a person's true centre! Listen to old recordings of Gandhi and you hear a voice that comes from the whole person. Listen to Nelson Mandela. The voice expresses the person; so you hear the person, not the voice. Then true communication takes place.

Chapter Twelve

When the pressure is on

It takes courage to grow up and become who you really are.

e. e. cummings

Vulnerability and stage fright

Your breath works naturally for you and expresses your inner intent when you are feeling at ease. When you are not, it becomes more difficult. Your breath is part of your whole system and when your state of mind is fearful or anxious the flow of breath is blocked and the voice is affected. This can be frustrating if you have worked on your voice and know that you can create a positive impact, only to lose it all when you feel tense or nervous. It can feel like a no-win situation to want to speak with your own voice and be authentic, but to know that being authentic involves showing your vulnerability in all its guises of shaking voice, lack of breath, high pitch or whatever other tricks nerves play on you.

Surveys in the US and the UK reveal that public speaking is the number one most feared activity. And it's not just the formal speech at a conference, dinner or wedding; people get nervous in many other communication situations such as meetings, interviews, "having it out" with a colleague or any "leadership moment" when they have the perception that what they want to say has a lot resting on it. Such moments can be a real challenge for people and create a lot of perspiration, anxiety and sleepless nights.

What is it like for you?

This book talks about being real and authentic, but when authentic means feeling utterly incompetent, no wonder we hide behind our role.

Look outward

A major gremlin in public speaking is your inner critical voice which can create havoc for your state of mind with its endless destructive monologue: "Look, your voice is shaking!" "People can see you're nervous." "People in your position shouldn't be nervous." "You're not up to the job. People can see that." "Oh no, my boss is in the audience, so now it's really important to create a good impression." "But you've forgotten what you're going to say, haven't you?" "This feels bad!"

As you enter or stand to present, you step over a threshold from private to public. So allow your eyes, ears and feeling sense to do the same. Step over the threshold and immediately direct your attention outward and away from your inner world.

First, switch your attention to the visual. You will do this most successfully with your eyes up. So raise your eyes and look out at your audience as you enter, and never let your head dip down as it does when you engage with internal dialogue. When you arrive at the podium or centre stage, look at everyone and speak. An audience enjoys direct eye contact. It gives them confidence in you which in turn helps to boost your own confidence.

Your other senses can assist your external focus too. Listen externally to the sounds in the room and outside. Feel the sensation of your toes touching the insides of your shoes. Smell the air in the room as you breathe deeply.

With your senses focused outward, you will be in the here and now, neither digging into your past for previous failures nor fearing future disasters. The audience will see you in the here and now and find it easy to relate to you.

Accept your nerves

"What! Of course I can't. If people see I'm nervous, I'm dead!"

Not true. Nervous energy is present in every great speaker's address, and particularly so at the beginning, if you really pay attention. Nerves are just energy, as excitement is energy. Call it nervous excitement. Once you accept that you are nervously excited and give up trying to hide it (not that you can completely anyway), you will find that the greatest cause of nerves has gone.

Accept. But don't go into stories. What does that mean? Accepting means that I am aware that my heart is beating fast and I accept that reality. Going into stories means that I am aware that my heart is beating fast and then I remember other occasions when this has happened and start to tell myself that this *means* that I am going to perform badly, that this *means* that I am going to trip over my words the way I did last time my heart beat fast, that this *means* that I am not adequate as a speaker and shouldn't be there at all.

It is the stories, not the feeling, that sabotage you. Every time a story comes into your head, let it go, and tell yourself, "I am enough. It's OK. I am enough."

Sarah's story

A friend phoned me one evening. "Can you help my colleague, Sarah," she asked. "She has an important conference on Friday week, and she's really worried about it."

I agreed readily and met Sarah the next day.

"I just get nervous before public speaking," she said. "And then my voice goes squeaky: I hate it."

"What, public speaking, or your voice?"

"Both!" She laughed. Sarah had quite a gentle voice that was easy to listen to.

"So, what happens to your voice," I asked.

"It just goes higher and squeaky," she sighed.

"Can you do that for me now?"

"Well, not really, I just go all tense." She screwed up her shoulders and drew them in. "And then I hate the sound of my voice so much that it happens even more." Her voice now sounded quite tense and strained.

"It sometimes feels as if someone else is talking, and my voice goes sort of echoey and unreal ..." She broke off as an unpleasant memory hit her. "It's really horrible," she finished abruptly.

"Have you ever lost it entirely," I asked.

"Only once," she replied. "I was still at school, and we had to give a talk on an assignment we'd been given. Mine was about some observations I'd made about plant life along the banks of a river near my home. I began OK but then made a mistake in the order of what I had decided to say, and when I opened my mouth to start the next sentence, I went blank. I didn't just forget what I was going to say. I forgot where I was, the reason for being there, *who* I was, who the audience was: it was all one big, white, terrifying blank. I was really scared. I've never forgotten it. I'm always worried that it will come back. It's like being frozen."

"It reminds me a little of a rabbit caught in the headlights of a car," I said. "You know that the way for the rabbit to be safe is for it to run, to get out of harm's way, but it doesn't have that instinct. It just freezes."

"That's me exactly," said Sarah. "I don't want to freeze, and it does me no good, but somehow I find myself doing it."

"So how would it be if you allowed yourself to move with the flow?" I asked.

"Well, that would be great, but I'm not sure that I would even know how to. And it would also feel like a risky strategy. It might all go pear-shaped."

"Do you know anyone whose delivery has an easy flow about it?"

"Well, not personally, but I really like the way Jonathan Ross on TV just keeps talking and chatting so easily. Whatever happens, he's just easy and flowing."

"If you were to 'put on' Jonathan's way of being, how he is in his body, how is that?"

Sarah giggled. "Well, I couldn't actually 'do' him—he sort of feels as if he's moving even when he's not … and he speaks before he thinks almost. Wow, that could get you into trouble!" She laughed and pulled a face.

"So, do him."

"Oh, I couldn't! He sort of …" Sarah leaned back in her chair and started to speak: "Well, ladies and gentlemen, I'm really pleased to have Oprah on the show tonight." She then burst into laughter. "Hey, he is a bit like that. It's quite easy." And she imitated some more.

"So what about it?" I asked. "What does he do that you don't?"

Sarah thought about it for a moment. "He uses all his energy," she reflected.

"Exactly. Energy is the answer: moving through your nerves. Stuck energy produces adrenalines and they poison your system. Moving energy quickly takes you beyond nerves. So before you speak, expend energy. Walk firmly up and down; feel the movement of every cell in your body, shake your hands vigorously, anything to get yourself moving. Then start dynamically. Look at everyone and smile and speak energetically."

"I don't like to look at people."

"You'll find it's OK. Walk firmly into the middle of the room, turn your eyes in a friendly way to me and then introduce yourself."

Sarah walked somewhat uncertainly, but she did look at me. Then she spoke quietly: "I'm Sarah Scott, and I'm going to give you this year's financial figures."

"Great," I said. "Now again, much more purposefully. Really smile at me and make my day. Energy in every cell of your body!"

Sarah did it again, and this time she marched in with a firm tread, smiled at me and began with lots of life in her delivery: "I'm Sarah Scott, and I'm really pleased to be with you today. And I have this year's figures for you!" Her voice came out surprisingly strongly and she was delighted.

"Hey, that's different. I really like that!"

"Isn't it amazing," I agreed. "Change the feeling and you change the voice. It's as simple as that."

A week later, Sarah phoned me excitedly. "The conference went really well," she exclaimed. "Not only was I much more energetic, but I also found I could think much more clearly, and I wasn't stuck in my notes as I used to be before. I'm on my way!"

Self-belief and sense of purpose

We talked about energy earlier, and the combination of relaxation (letting go) and energy is a powerful source of confidence.

Add to that your self-belief and sense of purpose: Why are you speaking? What's important about it? What matters to you? Answer these questions from your centre and you will come into your own voice. What do you want for yourself in this communication? What do you want for your listeners? What is your gift to them?

Where do you find the answers to these questions? Deep inside yourself. And it is deep inside yourself that you will feel the knowing that comes from having answers. That is the place to speak from. Sense where in your body you feel the answers are to be found. Feel the seed of your communication in that place and imagine the voice coming from there. Breathe and speak.

You are bigger than you think

We tend to think we will come across more powerfully as the CEO, head of sales, manager or figurehead than as ourselves, and therefore we act the role, without fully believing that we are big enough to fill it. The amount of effort we put into maintaining the role is in equal measure to the extent of our lack of belief. It is one of life's paradoxes that though the role might seem the most powerful aspect of the person, there is nothing, absolutely nothing that can compare to the power of someone coming across as herself.

Of course, it takes courage to let go of the role, so no wonder we hesitate. "One does not jump enthusiastically into being big: status can swallow every bit of your life energy," says African shaman, Malidoma Patrice Somé.[16] But in letting go, your inner genius and outer expression are aligned, and the increase in vitality and influence is phenomenal.

As yourself, you can be big. People get the best of you and your voice will be whatever you want it to be.

As Rachel Remen says in her inspirational collection of anecdotes, *My Grandfather's Blessings*:

> Living is a matter of passion and risk. Of finding something important and serving it ... of doing whatever is needed in order to live out loud.[17]

So what could be better? Let's all "live out loud"!

Chapter Thirteen

Two ways of being

A good head and a good heart are always a formidable combination.

Nelson Mandela

We have seen that your voice can express what is going on for you at a deeper level or it can simply fail to mirror your feeling and on the contrary actually disguise it. What is the difference in your state of mind between the two cases?

When your voice successfully expresses what is going on for you, you are present in the moment, experiencing and feeling in real time. When it is not expressing what is going on, there is a disconnect, a sense of being at one remove. It is like being present as an observer, looking on at everything that is happening, with your feelings locked away inside you. These are crucial distinctions in your way of relating to the present and they create fundamental differences to how you experience life and how you communicate. The choice of one or the other also affects your voice profoundly.

To discover more about these differences, I am going to give you an instruction now that I want you to follow without thinking about it too much.

Point to the "now".

Where did you point?

Many people point to their own body or to their own feet. "Now" is where they are: they stand in the now. They are *associated* into now.

Other people point to the ground just in front of themselves. "Now" is outside them. They are *dissociated* from the now.

You may have pointed somewhere else. Basically, if you pointed at your own body, you are associated into the moment. If you pointed somewhere outside your body, you are dissociated from the moment.

These two positions create different experiences, so let's experiment with them now.

Associating and dissociating

If you have found that your default position is associated into the now, start there, and experience fully how it is to be right in the present moment, looking out of your own eyes, aware of what you are feeling inside you.

Then take a step backwards, with the sense of leaving the present moment where you were standing a minute ago. Experience how it is to be dissociated, observing "you" from the outside. If you are already dissociated, step further backwards to put more distance between yourself and your feelings. Experience how that is, when you are at a remove from your feelings and emotions, looking on.

Then take a step even further back, to experience further detachment from the present. Notice how that is.

Then step forward again, step by step. And finally step into your own shoes in the now, fully experiencing how it is to be associated into all the feelings and sensations of the moment.

What have you learned about the two ways of being?

Association

> Her voice changed like a bird's:
> There grew more of the music, and less of the words.
>
> Robert Browning, "Flight of the Duchess"

As ways of being in the world, both association and dissociation have advantages. If you are associated into the moment, living from inside your body, you are particularly aware of all the feelings and emotions going on inside you. When you are having a good time, you are feeling all the pleasurable emotions in real time. When you are having a bad time, you are also aware of the painful emotions as they arise.

Equally, if you associate into a good memory from your past, you are right back there, present in that moment, looking out of your own eyes, and you feel again the pleasurable emotions of that time. If you associate into a bad time from your past, you imagine yourself back in that time, looking out of your own eyes, and you feel again the pain of that time.

Note that you can be associated for some memories and dissociated for others.

Dissociation

If you are dissociated from the present, you are outside the sensations of your body, looking on. When you are having a good time, you are aware of having a good time, but you do not feel the sensations of pleasure through your body. When you are having a bad time, you are able to distance yourself to an extent from the painful sensations of the moment.

If you dissociate from the good times you have had in the past, you will be able to remember them, but probably as a movie or picture, so you have the memory of pleasure at looking at yourself in the frame but do not relive the actual emotional sensations of pleasure. If you have a dissociated memory of a bad time in your past, you are able to remember the sights and sounds of that time, but distance yourself from them and avoid the unpleasant emotions in your body associated with the experience.

We have varying abilities to associate into some memories and dissociate from others. Clearly, associating into the good experiences and dissociating from the bad is a happy combination!

Now, how is this relevant to the voice? The free expressive voice that Kristin Linklater describes is an associated voice, where your feelings and emotions are naturally expressed as higher and lower resonance and all the other features of vocal variety. With the associated voice people hear the full range of your human experience, audible to them and vibrating in them through the sounds you make, and this gives you great potential to influence them. This is one of the elements of charisma, that elusive quality that so many speakers desire. The charismatic speaker is associated into the moment, vital and alive in her communication, creating a strong impact on her audience.

If you are dissociated as a default position, it will be difficult for you to create such an expressive voice. That was the case with Henry. I met him at a business meeting and as soon as I was introduced to him he started to talk to me about the opera. "Was at Covent Garden last night," he declared. "Performance of *Die Meistersinger*. Always a problem to get away from work for the 6 o'clock start, don't you find? Just love those five hour epics, don't you? Really test the stamina of the performers. Wonderful Hans Sachs on this occasion. Haven't heard better, not since Bayreuth in 2001. You know Bayreuth? Of course they have the room. Amazing stage space. But Sach's aria in the third act is the key, you know the one?"

I gave up the effort to take part in the conversation and listened to his voice, which had a dry, clipped quality and a relentless steady pace.

"Is that your favourite aria?" I ventured a while later.

"Best aria in the opera," he informed me. "Magnificent construction. Contains all the main themes. Requires amazing stamina of the singer of course."

"Is it very moving?" I enquired.

He looked at me askance. "Of course," he assured me in his clipped tones. "It's pivotal to the whole development of Sachs as a character."

I was beginning to be rather less than moved by his tones. Whatever he was asked, he answered with certainty like a textbook in that same dry voice. I was reminded of times I have sat through "Death by PowerPoint"[18] presentations at conferences, where the speaker has presented in steady confident tones so unvarying and unrelenting that my eyes have started to glaze over and the speaker's words have gradually faded to the rum-ti-ti-tum of the wheels as I snooze on a long train journey.

My reverie was interrupted by the arrival of a third party. "Hello Henry, hi Judy. You've met each other. You know Judy is a voice coach, Henry?"

Henry seemed interested. "I've done a lot of drama in my time," he confided. "Got to speak clearly and articulately. Just need to get people to listen to me. People just don't listen these days."

"We cover that in my course," I suggested. "Why don't you come and see what we do?" He chuckled and promised me that he would.

It is hard to continue listening to a voice like Henry's because, however interesting the content of what he has to say, the tone never varies and we have no idea of how he connects with what he has to say.

This happens when someone takes a step back from involvement in feeling and therefore the voice loses its connection with emotion. It separates head and body, and in dissociation the voice chooses to be allied with the head. Being dissociated is suitable for communicating non-emotional facts but isn't sufficient to convey the subtler shades of a communication. Without association into feeling the true voice cannot speak. Voice technique alone cannot provide the missing piece. Getting into feeling means associating into the body, so association is the route to more expressive communication.

I didn't see Henry again that year. But eighteen months later, before his daughter got married, he came to see me privately to have couple of sessions on his wedding speech. We got to talking about dissociated voices.

"It happens quite frequently in business," I explained, "where a senior manager will adopt a persona of authority—and the voice that goes with it—as soon as he crosses the threshold each day. In most cases the voice usually relaxes when work people are safely out of earshot. But if this kind of dissociated voice was learned early in life, it can become permanent."

"What's wrong with that?" challenged Henry.

"There's nothing wrong with it, but a voice created like that always lacks the colour and life of a spontaneous voice. It just stays the way it is. Nothing changes its tones."

It's hard for people like Henry to recognise how they are lacking the opportunity to communicate genuinely in their speech. When I next saw him almost a year later he told me that he'd been shocked by what I said.

"Then my father died," he said. He was ill for several months and I saw quite a lot of him. He said things he'd never said before. And I did too." He coloured and his voice was softer. "And I realised for the first time what you were talking about too."

Henry discovered the key for getting people to listen. He had to reveal *himself*, step into what he was actually feeling and experiencing at the time. That is exactly what it means to associate into the body.

"I never realised", he said, "that other people really can detect how you are dealing with life from your voice. I always thought that a professional voice convinced everybody. But it doesn't, does it? Not if it's only skin deep."

Advantages of each way of being

The dissociated voice is fine for some communication. But if you want to be able to speak using the full range of your voice, you will want to learn to associate. Then you have the potential to influence others with your voice.

Speaking in an associated way presents you with a new challenge. With feeling and emotion may come an increased sensation of fear. You may be more in the moment than someone who is dissociated but, in the process of being so, you may also feel more vulnerable and scared. Of course, any of us can feel fear, for example when we have a challenging presentation to make, and we have already discussed strategies for dealing with it. But, if you are naturally associated in the moment, not only are you likely to be more aware of the sensations of fear in your body, you may also feel the fear of involuntarily disclosing feelings that you don't want others to see. So you are not only experiencing negative feelings but also negative feelings *about* those feelings.

You always have the choice to step out of the moment and become dissociated. One of the advantages of detachment from an unpleasant emotion is the possibility of thinking more clearly. Many speakers communicate from this space at all times. It keeps emotion at a distance and therefore can feel safer, but the downside is the sacrifice of expressions of warmth, intensity, determination and compassion, indeed much that connects human beings powerfully and makes communication satisfying.

So there are advantages and disadvantages to each way of being. Stepping in (associating) allows you to be alive and to connect well. Stepping out (dissociating) is a useful skill for assessing a situation, taking stock, checking time or recovering your equilibrium should the need arise.

Speak while associated and dissociated

You will have found out from the previous exercise whether you feel most comfortable associated or dissociated.

Begin to make a speech, either associated or dissociated, whichever is most comfortable for you. Continue for a minute or so.

Then, if you are associated, step back to dissociate. Leave all the feelings in the associated space and gain a sense of distance from them. Carry on speaking from that detached place. If dissociated, step forward as if you are stepping into your own body to look out of your own eyes, and get in touch with the feelings in your body and the emotional energy of what you want to communicate. Continue your speech for a few minutes more from the new perspective.

Notice the differences. They can be many and surprisingly marked!
Record the session with a video camera to see for yourself. Or get
verbal feedback from someone.

In general, being associated into the moment will allow you to
come across more dynamically as a speaker. Dissociating from
the immediate experience from time to time allows you to make
detached observations, and to gain perspective on timings, group
dynamics, the energy of the audience and so on, to support you as
you speak associated into the moment. If your feelings are overwhelming, dissociating can give you a breather and the sense of
being more in control.

If you want to lead and inspire people, you will want to be associated into the moment much of the time you are communicating.
People will respond much more readily. As we have seen, you can
fake the difference: put on more energy, shout, laugh and act with
confidence. But in this case, true connection will elude you. The
influential voice shows strength, caring, determination, softness,
playfulness—and all these energies come through you to touch an
audience only if you are associated into them.

The ability to be associated is a major hidden ability of great speakers. The richly varied vibrations of the associated voice literally
create similar vibrations within the listener, and create a connection that does not happen by other means.

A more spacious way of being

We have explored association and dissociation with the concept of
"stepping in" and "stepping out". There is another way to achieve
authenticity without sacrificing control, where, instead of stepping
out when you feel vulnerable or sense that emotions are inappro-
priate or unmanageable, you have the sensation of expanding your
associated centre, to give yourself more space to breathe and be. In
this way, you remain very much in the moment, and connected to
your core, but give yourself a wider perspective and greater objec-
tivity when you need it.

Expand your centre

Associate into the moment, as you did before, and then, from that feeling place, become aware of your centre just below your solar plexus, and tune into awareness of that place, breathing steadily. When you feel calm and centred in the present moment, imagine that this centre expands outwards, getting bigger and bigger, till it extends beyond you. Keep breathing, focusing on your sense of the centre as you breathe in, and relaxing and expanding as you breathe out. It's a feeling of standing in an expanded place, as if you have a larger aura.

If you then speak from that expanded place, you will find that your voice comes from your centre. You will be speaking from the whole of you. At the same time, you have more space and time for thinking, so it will feel calmer. You will have more access to spontaneous thought and can translate that straight into speech.

If your feelings are unpleasant or overwhelming as you stand associated in your centre, say to yourself, "I am *more* than this", as you expand your sense of centre.

Standing in the middle of this expanded place is like being in the eye of the storm, the still centre. In this place, you are very present, not detached, but you are in a place of stillness, where your feelings cannot overwhelm you.

Part Five

Your Voice Is You

Chapter Fourteen

Energy and intention

Playing the role

There are no right voices and wrong voices. There are just voices that affirm the truth of the moment and voices that hide the truth. So how much of yourself do you allow to be expressed through your voice?

You can usually detect that a person is dissociated through the flatness of tone. It often also means that the person is playing a role, even though they may not be aware of it. You can spot a presenter in "professional" role in business presentations: there are three easy ways to tell. Firstly, the presenter's physiology has an element of stiffness, however slight, in the upper body, almost as if their shoulders were carrying epaulettes as part of the uniform of office. Secondly, the voice often has the bland pleasant quality I described earlier, or an artificial energetic quality, which reveals nothing of more subtle inner energy, emotion or connection. Thirdly, and the easiest to notice, you find yourself after a while failing to be engaged with the process, however professional, experienced or upbeat the speaker appears to be. Ultimately, you get bored.

As a senior police officer reminded me once, there are times when it is appropriate to speak in role and not allow your listener access to you as a person. When he is interrogating a suspect, it is most useful for him to leave "self" out of the equation and communicate as an official figure. But if you are speaking as a leader, you will be significantly more influential if you are present as a person as well as in your title. When you speak from your role—as managing director, CEO, director, whatever it might be—a proportion of your energy goes into maintaining the role and the audience does not quite experience you directly and authentically. Let us be clear, this is not the difference between talking about yourself or not; it is about being there with 100 per cent of you available to use your creativity and wisdom to respond to the situation rather than just you in your official role.

So if you are consulted as a professional—whether therapist, hypnotherapist, doctor, counsellor or consultant—where clearly you are communicating in an official capacity, *even so* you will have most influence if you do not hide your vulnerability behind the fortress of the title, but appear entirely present in all your humanity.

Hal Milton in *Going Public* describes the difference:

> When you posture yourself, you are using energy to force your muscles to act in a certain way. If your structure is aligned and balanced, there is nothing to do with your posture. The structurally supported body conserves energy and creates a feeling of lightness and "upness". The posturing body, with habitual holding patterns, reflects attitudes and also creates emotions and perceptions, congruent with the holding posture of the body. [19]

Carlos Castaneda in *The Art of Dreaming* gives us a glimpse of even grander possibilities, if we are fully available:

> If we were capable of losing some of that importance, two extraordinary things would happen to us. One, we would free our energy from trying to maintain the illusory idea of our grandeur; and two, we would provide ourselves with enough energy to ... catch a glimpse of the actual grandeur of the universe. [20]

When the speaker is authentic, her intention is transformed through breath straight into expression, and her energy connects directly with the listener. Her body has a natural ease about it: you sense that she is at ease with herself, comfortable in her own skin. And her words arouse a feeling in you, beyond rational agreement. You are *moved* in some way; there is *motion* in you. You feel physically and mentally energised by the communication.

When we think about the energy of the spoken word, we may think in terms of mental energy. But the energy field for the voice is your whole body: once you become aware of the aliveness of feeling in your body as well as the alertness of your mind, you connect with your life force, and can then connect energetically with other people.

Feel the energy

Hold your hands facing each other, about 15 cm apart and feel the subtle sensation of aliveness, like a tingling, in them. Move your hands gently closer together, and then further apart. Feel the energy running between them. That is one expression of your life force.

Smile with your body

Now think of something that gives you joy: perhaps the memory of a beautiful place, or a joyful occasion, or a person who loves you. Feel the pleasure inside you and expand that pleasure inside your body, as if it were a giant smile spreading across your chest. Or, "smile with your buttocks", as I was once told! There is your life force too: a warm inner energy available to you.

Inner energy

> He whose face gives no light, shall never become a star.
>
> William Blake

Your inner personal energy makes an enormous difference to the sound and vitality of your voice. It's not just the difference between being enthusiastic and lethargic. It is about being "switched on", your mind and emotions connected to your delivery. When you possess this energy, people hear the live intention in your voice; when your engagement is low, the voice becomes lacklustre and boring.

The old customer care slogan, "Have a nice day", is a typical example of a phrase that can be meaningful or empty depending on the energy behind it. The energy comes from the strength of your intention. You can say "Have a nice day" in a bright cheery voice without a genuine wish behind it, and it sounds synthetic and pointless. When you express a genuine desire, the phrase comes to life and influences the other person positively.

The listener sees a difference in the aliveness of your features, in the light in your eyes, for instance. But they will hear the difference clearly too. Listen for yourself to the difference between someone talking to you with the energy that comes from passion for their subject and someone telling you about something that doesn't engage them in the slightest.

Speak with passion

Speak for two or three minutes about a subject that you are passionate about: a place or a person or animal you love, a hobby that excites you, or something that really matters to you.

Record yourself or preferably do the exercise with someone and take it in turns to speak. Notice how the increased internal energy when you are passionate about something affects the sound of your voice. Take note of the voice tone, rhythm, speed, variation and so on.

Now, each speak about a subject which you find tedious. Attempt to use the same way of speaking that you used for your passionate speech. Notice how even with your attempt to sound the same as the first time, it sounds less authentic.

Of course, there are times in a professional context when you may want to engage other people in a subject that does not particularly interest you. In order to harness your energy whatever the occasion and subject matter, you need to find some elements in your subject that you *can* connect with. You might not feel passionate about the latest performance initiative but you can perhaps feel passionate about its effects on people, or your desire for improvement, or some other element. Even when the subject completely bores you, there is always the opportunity presented by the connection with the people you are talking to: you can want to give them a good time, keep them interested, feel a connection with them. When you focus internally on any of these energetic elements your speaking voice will come alive.

Energy for public speaking

Voice is vibration. Free vibration from free breath involves the whole of you and connects with other people at the level of wholeness. You "find your voice", you "sing your own tune" and others are influenced by how you sound.

This energetic connection happens whenever you are authentic and in contact with your inner self. But if you are speaking to a large group of people or in a large space there is an advantage to generating an even higher energy to cross the larger distances.

The increase in energy also helps with performance anxiety. If you are nervous, much of your energy can be bound up in dealing with that: coping with the run of inner talk, taking physical control of trembling, combating the feeling of self-consciousness. One of the best preparations you can make for a public presentation is to get your energy flowing, as we saw in the section on physical energy preparation in Chapter 9.

Many professional actors and singers encounter their worst nerves when they are required to appear in public, not in role but as themselves. Their job requires them to act a part; and appearing as themselves can arouse a sense of vulnerability that is not present when acting as someone else. Watch a well-known actor or singer when he is interviewed in public. Often he will heighten his energy as a strategy to overcome nerves. When he first appears with the interviewer he starts on a highly energetic level which can come across as flamboyant, but this abundance of energy gradually settles down as he becomes more comfortable. It's better to hit the ground running in this way than to hold on in an attempt to control nerves, and come across as stiff and lifeless for the whole interview.

In the flow

> Do not fail
> To learn from
> The pure voice of an
> Ever-flowing mountain stream
> Splashing over the rocks.
>
> Morihei Ueshiba, founder of Aikido, *The Art of Peace*

When you are fully present in your body and relaxed your concentration becomes focused and the abundant force of your energy is released. This energy is felt as life and power in your inner core, and allows that vital part of you—which you might be tempted to hide from a sense of vulnerability—to connect with your listeners.

People with charisma glow with inner energy more than other people. This is very different from manic energy, busyness or quick thinking. It is more a sensation of being fully awake: awake in the head and thinking, awake and open in the heart and feeling, awake and centred in the gut and intuition, awake in the whole body. Being present in the here and now you become a speaker who has presence.

This state of mental and physical aliveness is sometimes referred to as being "in flow" or "in the zone". In many fields of endeavour those who excel know how to access this state. They describe it in various ways.

Recalling the creation of his monumental oratorio *The Messiah* in an amazing twenty-four days, Handel told a friend, "Whether I was in the body or out of my body when I wrote it, I know not. ... I think I did see all Heaven before me and the great God Himself." [21]

In the field of sports, the tennis player Lleyton Hewitt described the state of flow in a media interview after producing some of his best tennis ever in a Wimbledon match: "Everything became amazingly easy," he said: "It was like the ball was as big as a football and just couldn't miss the centre of the racquet: I felt I couldn't do anything wrong." [22]

The state of flow is also sometimes reached when we have expended all our conscious reserves and surrendered to the powers of the unconscious. The coach Tim Gallwey tells of a time when his car broke down in freezing ice and snow, many miles from habitation. Setting out on foot, he became aware that if he walked he was likely to freeze before he could reach help, but when he ran he became too exhausted to continue. Death from freezing stared him in the face. At that point, he surrendered himself to whatever was to happen, and through surrender entered a place of flow where his energy suddenly became limitless:

172

I began walking calmly down the road, suddenly aware of the
beauty of the night. I became absorbed in the silence of the
stars and in the loveliness of the dimly lit forms around me;
everything was beautiful. Then without thinking, I started
running. To my surprise I didn't stop for a full forty minutes,
and then only because I spotted a light burning in the window
of a distant house.[23]

Students of various spiritual and philosophical systems of the
world have learnt how to harness this energy flow. Japanese Ki,
Chinese Qi, Mana from Huna, Wilhelm Reich's Orgone or bio-
energy and Prana in Yoga all describe a life force energy available to us all. Harnessing your inner energy depends on breath.
These mostly ancient practices all involve tapping into the energy
through better breathing. So, study of any of these practices can be
a powerful way to get in touch with your inner energy and thus
directly with your authentic voice.

Your full voice comes from the sense of live movement in the
breath. The feeling is very different from the typical way of being
"alive" in busy Western society. In the West, many of us live a life
that yo-yos between electric tension and lifeless droop. At times in
the day we are running full-pelt in the stressful busyness of daily
life, aware of the myriad thoughts in our head and vaguely aware
of the tension in our bodies. At other times, we are slumped in
front of the television pretty much unaware of anything. Neither of
these states is particularly good for us: the one strains our physical
and mental resources and the other does little to restore them. And
neither permits us to breathe fully. The alive state, on the other
hand, is beautifully relaxed but also elastic, flexible and awake
with the breath: ready for anything.

When you combine the sense of aliveness with what you know
about resonance you can decide where you want to speak from.
Speak as though it is the body that talks, not the head. Before you
speak think about the part of your body that is most involved in
what you have to say. For example, if you are expressing an opinion, think of the sound coming from your chest.

Think of your voice as existing in the silence before you speak.
The energy of what you are going to say comes in the breath and
silence before the sound. The energy for the sound is already there,

so you can then just allow the sound to happen. Rehearsing your voice in silence is a good way to prepare for speaking well.

Try it out in the following exercise.

Rehearse in silence

Put your attention to where your sound is going to come from and hear inside your body the voice you want to produce.

For example, for the voice of the gut, imagine the whole-bodied sound, the deep resonance. Get the feeling of how it is to speak in that voice.

Feel the energetic impulse to communicate, and breathe into this sensation.

Then, with the complete feeling of this experience, allow the voice to be heard fully out loud.

Sounds good?

Connecting to your inner energy is a central piece of speaking influentially. Here is a breathing practice that most people find calming. It's a good one to practise at a time when you want to be serene, centred and prepared—before giving a talk or speech for instance. It will work best if you can get someone to read it to you or record your own voice reading the words and play that back. Then you can just focus on your breathing and nothing else.

Breathe into your centres

First, relax your body and mind, and tune into a sense of stillness and aliveness.

Sigh out completely, out loud, letting your body relax fully, and then breathe in fresh air. Do this a couple of times, feeling your whole body involved gently with the emptying and filling of air. Then start to breathe slowly into different parts of your body; you can take two or three breaths in each part. As you breathe, be aware of the energy that enters each part of your body as you breathe, as follows.

First, when you breathe in, pay attention to your belly, feeling the air fill that part of your body, and being aware of your grounded, centred self and the powerhouse of energy in that place. Breathe out, aware of renewed relaxation. Repeat the slow in-breath with attention focused on your belly, and the slow out-breath relaxing more and more. Repeat the whole breath two or three times.

Then breathe the air gently into the area of your heart and feel the warmth of feeling and compassion that is associated with that place in your body. As you breathe out, sense the warm feeling extending out into the world. Repeat two or three times.

Then breathe into your chest; place your attention there and feel the strength of that area of your body. As you breathe out feel the strength that will allow you to accomplish what you want in the world. Repeat as before.

Next, breathe in with awareness of your throat. Feel a soft relaxation there and be aware of your desire to communicate, and the permission you give yourself to speak your truth. As you breathe out, release any tension you feel there. Repeat as before.

Then breathe in with an awareness of the air filling your head, your sinuses, the spaces behind your nose, cheeks and ears and particularly the space between your eyes, and feel the lively energy and zest for life that belongs here. As you breathe out release your fun, enthusiasm and energy into the world. Repeat as before.

Finally, breathe in and out a few times with an awareness of your whole body as it moves with the breath.

Chapter Fifteen

Last word

A bird doesn't sing because it has an answer, it sings because it has a song.

Maya Angelou

Living voice

You can talk *about* something or alternatively you can use your voice to *express* something. When you talk about something the words do the work. The intention is for the listener to take in the words, as they would the words in a book, and make meaning from those words. When someone crafts a speech with care, and then says the words of that speech, this is the intention. But when you address an audience, you cannot *not* communicate with your tone of voice and body language as well. Your words when spoken live always contain additional meaning and nuance that comes from *how* you communicate. This is the public speaker's special concern and opportunity.

Your voice is alive. Every word starts with breath, and breath is not only a physical vibration; it is also an inner energy, a spiritual vibration. The dance teacher Gabrielle Roth talks about being "grounded in our body, pure in our heart, clear in our mind, rooted in our soul, and suffused with the energy, the spirit of life."[24] We all have this remarkable instrument, the voice, which has the capacity to connect with the life within us. And this is what gives it such power to stir others' lives. Sound emerges from the depth of our being, and its vibrations touch the depth of another's being. Travelling deep inside, it rouses the heart and stimulates a response within the hearer.

I want to suggest that influence works most often at this level: not on the surface alone, at the level of the actual words and their meaning, but below the surface at the level of energy. The word "influence" (*influere*—"to flow into") illustrates the process. When you influence, you join with someone's energy by "flowing into" it, and then it is the power of your energy or "life force", your way of being, that affects the other person. They are changed energetically, emotionally, by this force, which is expressed very much in the voice—strong voice, caring voice or passionate voice.

Now, it would be more reasonable to suggest that we are influenced by the content of someone's words, and of course this happens. You say something that makes good sense to me, and I am influenced by your remarks. But this happens perhaps to a lesser extent than we like to think. We are more used to *resisting* the power of others' logic when it questions our own opinions and beliefs, and especially when the arguments are delivered strongly.

Forceful speech is common in today's world. We live in the age of the sound bite. Human beings vie with one other to sway public opinion. Buy my goods! Vote for me! Agree with me! Follow me! Communication opportunities have exploded into websites, email, blogs and ever more ingenious means of advertising. Speeches are pre-written and addresses recited from autocue. But whenever human communication is prepared, mechanised and calculated, even though it might seem energetic superficially, the energy is robotic, the effect unsurprising, and it fails to stir us. I know within a fraction of second when a phone call comes from a recorded voice: its synthetic energy and lack of subtlety give it away and I slam the phone down in an instant.

There is no substitute for living speech. Greek orators knew it and our current politicians and thought leaders know it still. People are highly influenced by communication that, whether recorded or pre-planned or not, is created with a spontaneous energy. In political races, voters are more influenced by a politician's conference speech than by his executive skills, and more impressed by unplanned comments than by calculated statements. The most expressively read prepared communication does not achieve the impact of an off-the-cuff remark coming from a genuine impulse to communicate. The living voice expresses a person's state of mind and therefore expresses in sound far more than the person says.

Vibrating in tune

> Oh, there is something in that voice that reaches
> The innermost recesses of my spirit!
>
> Henry Wadsworth Longfellow, *Christus*

As we have seen, the voice is like the Indian bell that rings true when held freely but makes an unsatisfactory clack when held tightly. When you contradict the meaning of your words in the way you say them, or speak in contradiction with your own being, then the listener hears discordant or shallow sounds which upset or confuse. But when you are in tune with the meaning of your words and your energy is flowing unimpeded, expressing what all parts of you want to express, your sound reverberates and moves the listener.

In terms of vibration, when you speak in tune with your being your vibration sets up a complementary vibration in the other person. You can illustrate this process with two tuning forks. When you strike one and set it beside the other, the second fork begins to sound in resonance with the first. The two forks are "on the same wavelength".

When you speak on the same wavelength as another person, without psychological blocks, disguise or deceit, the vibrations of your voice can be a source of strength, gentleness and humour for them. Being in tune with yourself, you free up the body from its mental blocks and your voice comes from your internal energy or life force. If you are in tune with the best of you, the best of you will emerge in your voice and others will benefit from what you have to offer. Then your words become truly powerful. You can affect others at the level of their being. In this world of vibrating energy, you can use your voice to vibrate in tune with yourself and the universe: an awesome possibility and responsibility.

The power of sound

> He who knows the secret of sound, knows the mystery of the whole Universe.
>
> Hazrat Inayat Khan

The field of cymatics gives us powerful scientific examples of the effects of sound. When sounds are played or sung in the vicinity of powder or sand placed on a disc, the sound vibrations move the particles on the disc, which dance themselves into a pattern. The waves of sound literally create forms.

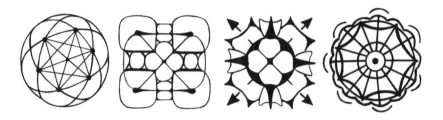

Examples of patterns formed by sound

The Swiss natural scientist, Hans Jenny, carried out some beautiful experiments about fifty years ago to show how musical sounds create regular patterns. As the frequency rose the image kept the pattern up to a certain point, and then rapidly changed to a new configuration, more complex and intricate than the previous one. The images thus formed are truly awe-inspiring, including geometrical shapes, butterflies and mandala-like patterns. What we can see in the sand patterns is a visual representation of the graceful and cohesive effect of sounds on our bodies and minds. What is particularly interesting from the point of view of the voice is that discordant sounds fail to produce these beautiful effects.

Sounds affect us on every level—physical, emotional and spiritual. Sounds that affect us harmoniously are often sounds that we consider sacred. There are numerous stories through history about the powerful and healing effects of sound. In legend, the god Orpheus could calm the guard-dog of hell and tame the deadly voices of the Sirens with his lyre. Some traditions say that the world was brought into being by sound. "In the beginning was the Word" are the first words of St John's Gospel. "Nada Brahma"—the world is sound—says the ancient Sanskrit. Certain meditation techniques use the sound "aum", which vibrates through the chanter's body to create a state of calm awareness. Discordant jarring sounds, on the other hand, can affect us negatively, create internal imbalance and raise stress levels.

"I want to utilize sound, resonance, vibration, to bring people closer to their own hearts," said the guitar virtuoso, Carlos Santana. Research is growing into the transformative and healing energy of sound. Harmonic sounds can induce a feeling of calm in us or raise us to great heights of emotion. Tuneful sound is used to maintain health, to heal disease and to restore balance and harmony to people's lives.

A society that suppresses forthright, honest voices cannot progress in human terms. We need people that speak their internal truth to us. And if this is to happen in the world, each one of us has a quest to find our own voice. Every one of us needs to know that there is no other voice like ours, and that each of us has a voice to be heard. As the creative dancer and choreographer Martha Graham memorably affirmed:

> There is a vitality, a life force, an energy, a quickening that is translated through you into action, and because there is only one of you, in all of time, this expression is unique. If you block it, it will never exist through any other medium and it will be lost—the world will not have it. You must keep that channel open. It is not for you to determine how good it is, nor how valuable. Nor how it compares with other expressions. It is for you to keep it yours—clearly and directly.[25]

Find your voice

> Words mean more than what is set down on paper. It takes the human voice to infuse them with shades of deeper meaning.
>
> Maya Angelou

So the study of voice is also a journey back to yourself. What may have begun as a simple search for increased clarity or impact in communication turns you inside in search of yourself. It is a true hero's journey, leading you to fight the demons of your own blocks and hinders in the quest for your true voice, and like the archetypal quest described by T. S. Eliot in "Little Gidding", the exploration brings you to arrive where you started and know the place for the first time. In finding your voice, you find yourself.

The voice that you discover is beautiful in its transparency. Here is the paradox. If you try to create a "beautiful" voice, you miss the target; if you aim for transparent, alive communication, for "truth in sound", your voice sounds beautiful and uniquely yours. And you find that you have something to say.

What does your own voice tell you about the state of your feelings and soul? We see the process of "finding a voice" in many of the great artists and musicians. Look at the paintings of Picasso from youth to old age and you go through many fine paintings that echo other painters, and finally reach the Picasso who has "found his voice". The paintings become uniquely his, unlike anyone else's on earth. You see the same process in a composer like Mozart. His youthful pieces could be by many other fine composers of his day but his final *Requiem* could be by no one but him. The wide-ranging sympathy, the combination of sorrow and tenderness together with touches of lightness and even humour, could only be Wolfgang Amadeus Mozart.

Like so much learning, "finding your voice" becomes more simple and literal the more you examine the phrase. When you find the natural power of your physical voice, you discover how to express your way of being in the world and as a result you find your meta-phorical voice in the world and people listen to you.

There's a story from the Hasidic tradition about the Rabbi Susya. Shortly before his death he tells his students, "When I get to heaven, they will not ask me, 'Why were you not Moses?' but 'Why were you not Susya? Why did you not become what only you could become?' "

"Be your note", says the medieval poet Rumi:

> Be your note
> I'll show you how it is enough.
> Go up on the roof at night
> in this city of the soul.
> Let everyone climb on their roofs
> And sing their notes!
> Sing loud!

Finding your voice requires you both to listen to your inner voice and to find its expression on the outside. Your voice works not only inter-personally with other people but also intra-personally within yourself. When you live too much in the intellect—your head—you lose connection with your own feelings and with others, and you lose depth in your voice. When you accept yourself and give yourself permission to express the real you, then head and heart are joined. There is a flow between heart and head through the vocal cords, and your inner voice connects harmoniously with outward expression. You can use your voice more fully, letting it flow from greater depths.

Working on your voice is an exciting journey, for it reveals facets of yourself that need to emerge for successful leadership. In the authentic chest voice people perceive your strength. In your heart voice, they hear your caring and passion. In your head voice they hear your enthusiasm and humour. In your voice of the gut they hear your wholeness and deep intuition. Developing your voice is a physical learning—breathing, posture and relaxation are all important—but it is equally a learning of mind, heart and spirit. When body, mind, heart and spirit are integrated the positive, balanced leadership of self that emerges creates success in every system of its endeavour: in organisation, corporation, team and family. You "find your voice" in the deepest sense.

So finding your voice is also the way to *have* a voice in the world. In accepting yourself, you present a solid self for others to connect with. They can say, *I see you, I hear you, I sense you.* And what is it that they sense? They sense the connection to your roots, a connection to something more profound in the deep well of your being. They sense your strength and grounded centre. They sense the warmth in your heart. They sense the fun and excitement of your connection with the earth and sky and the heavens. In your voice they hear *you*.

Appendix

Voice troubleshooting

These additional notes are called "troubleshooting" but it's good to remember that using your voice is actually excellent for your health. Vocalising energises you; it improves your breathing and your circulation; it stimulates your brain; it warms your heart and spirit. It delays old age. According to Victoria Meredith, professor at the University of Western Ontario, who used the university's adult choirs for her research, participation in choral music leads to increased respiratory function, better circulation, a heightened immune system, improved brain function and improved overall health.

It is a wonderful truth that when you learn how to influence others *from a centred place within yourself*, voice problems largely become a thing of the past. When you use your whole body to speak, it stays in balance, and responds by serving you well.

I have included this Appendix for those times when you need extra help and also to suggest some good practices for looking after your voice. Many of the suggestions in this chapter have been dealt with more fully elsewhere in the book, and in these cases I have indicated where to look for a more detailed explanation.

First, let's look at some common voice problems and how to solve them.

How can I avoid my voice getting tired?

Learn how to produce your voice correctly!

OK, that is easily said, but in fact everything you have learned in this book will help your voice to stay healthy. Faulty production puts a strain on the voice, so learning how to breathe well and produce your voice more naturally is the best way of preventing voice problems. Singers with a sound technique, who consistently produce their voices well, continue to have youthful and robust-sounding voices well into their eighties and beyond; whereas auctioneers who have relentlessly pounded their voices without training or club performers who have forced their voices against loud background noise in smoky atmospheres for years often have hoarse or damaged voices before they reach middle age.

Remember that in speaking well *the body* assumes the energetic responsibility for producing the voice, not the vocal cords. So breathing and relaxing are important to enable your body to play its full part. As we have seen, the actual *source* of the energy is psychic, in that the impulse to speak comes from internal energy—desire to communicate, emotion and so on—not from physically pushing the vocal cords into action.

Start your voice smoothly

Some of us start every sentence with a kind of glottal stop, which hits the vocal cords with a bang. You can hear this effect in others when every sentence starts with a loud "Uh!" To notice the difference, try starting a sentence with a gentle onset. In singing, it is called singing "on the breath". To start any sentence without hitting your vocal cords, try the following:

Speaking "on the breath"

Imagine in your mind's eye a view that pleases you.

Breathe in deeply, and then begin to breathe out again.

When your breath is half-way expelled, allow sound to emerge from the breath, and say something about the view you are imagining, e.g. "That's amazing", or "What a wonderful place to be", or some other comment that arises naturally out of what you are imagining.

The aim is to change breath into sound seamlessly in one continuous flow.

Speak at the pitch that is comfortable for you

The pitch that is most natural for you will depend on your physiology, and your voice will sound at its best if you speak at the pitch that is most comfortable. If you try to speak too high or too low for any length of time your voice will be under strain and will eventually sound tired. You can easily hear examples in the media of presenters who have artificially lowered their voices to sound more authoritative, and the effect is artificial as well as being tiring for them.

Find your most comfortable pitch

Take a breath, and sigh deeply, comfortably and out loud.

The pitch of your sigh will be a good pitch for your natural voice. After sighing out loud, say a few words at the same pitch.

Give your voice a break!

Your voice needs a chance to recover if you use it a lot. The most beautiful voice requires breaks of silence. The vocal cords love a bit of quiet!

And if the voice does get tired ...

Let go, relax. You can strain the voice easily if you are feeling stressed. Parts of your body stiffen up and the voice does not have the freedom to work so well. If you ignore this, and just push the voice out anyhow, you are liable to do damage. So breathe out and let go of the tension, move your neck, shoulders and upper body.

The jaw is a common place for problems. This hinge gets used many thousands of times a day and sometimes it just needs time out to recover. If the bottom half of your face becomes uncomfortable at any time, just realise that the muscles have tensed up, and if possible give your voice a rest for a while.

There is an easy exercise for the jaw in Chapter 5.

How can I avoid sounding nasal?

Sometimes you sound nasal when you have a common cold or because your nose is blocked, and this is just a temporary condition.

In any case, resonating in the nose isn't all bad. Nasal resonance is one element of what actors call using the "mask", which creates brilliance and carrying power in the voice. If you place your voice up in the cheekbones and nose, it resounds with great intensity in that small concave space, and can be heard in the largest room with little effort. So this can be helpful as one aspect of resonance.

Test your nasal resonance

To test the resonating qualities of a concave space, try facing into the corner of a room at a distance of about 10–20 cm and speaking into the corner with your normal voice. The resonance is powerful, isn't it? That is the kind of effect you achieve by resonating into the front of your head including the nose.

But not on its own!

If, however, you drive *all* the sound into your nose, by bunching up your tongue at the back and being lazy with your soft palate, the resulting sound is powerful, monotonous and hard on the ear. It dominates everything and is just not pleasant to listen to. Depending on the pitch, your voice will sound adenoidal, strident or piercing, and completely devoid of emotional subtlety.

Remedies for nasal sound

To change a chronic nasal voice you probably need a voice therapist. But you can also try the following:

Use your breath more actively. The nasal voice comes from lazy breath. Just as a freeing exercise, practise speaking with a breathy voice to feel the sensation of air moving.

Work on using your other resonators to restore the balance of your voice, as described in Chapter 6.

Relax. Open your mouth more, right inside and far back, as you do when you yawn. Move your mouth and jaw more.

Yawning is wonderfully good for you and your voice. You increase your intake of air when you yawn. You naturally stretch all your face muscles. You give your speaking apparatus a spontaneous workout!

Become more aware of your inner energy. The impulse to speak comes from your thoughts and emotions. Keep those alive as you feel the desire to form words.

Sigh with sound. Feel the glorious relaxation of sound that has no effort in it, that just comes from breath and a feeling of wellbeing. Sigh and then speak from the same place.

More serious conditions

Sometimes a nasal voice is due to other causes, such as adenoid problems, a nasal polyp or tumour, a deviated septum or chronic sinusitis. Of course, these need to be checked out with a doctor.

How can I avoid hesitating and stuttering?

This problem presents itself in varying degrees of severity. Many of us stutter or stammer a bit when we feel daunted or when we are unsure of what we are going to say.

Many of us too, without having a serious stutter, have adopted the habit of a stumbling manner of speech, full of "ums" and "ers" and false starts and hesitations. If this is your style, try the following.

Support your voice with the breath

If you breathe in a hurry, high up in your chest, you will not take in enough air to support a sentence and your words will come out in a rush to get your point across before you run out of air. When you breathe habitually in this way, you may not even be aware of the cause of your scurries, half-breaths and "ums" and "aahs". Shortage of air is a very likely reason. The hesitations are little subconscious cues to grab a tiny bit more air.

So, learn how to breathe properly! Good breathing will iron out a surprising number of problems to do with lack of fluency. See Chapter 4 on breathing.

Slow down

> The trouble with talking too fast is you may say something you haven't thought of yet.
>
> Ann Landers

Forcing yourself to slow down will often cure the stumbling that comes from immediate tension and uncertainty. Anxiety about getting the words out at all will often cause you to hurry and snatch at the words. Slowing down can feel counter-intuitive but if you do, you will have more time to order your thoughts and will naturally find ways to improve the breathing to sustain the slower pace.

Clarify what you want to say

Knowing what you want to say doesn't necessarily imply that you have to have a fully formed sentence in your head before you open your mouth. Many of us think as we speak, and this is fine. But if your thinking is muddled, your speech will be hesitant. Clear thinking will usually produce clear articulation.

Get used to formulating a whole concept in your mind *before* you open your mouth. This will involve taking more pauses between sentences, and in general means slowing down *in your head*!

If you have a quick brain that constantly rushes on to the next thing, and easily spots exceptions, caveats, new details and fresh twists to your theme, this will need some practice. Newsreaders have ample practice in squeezing the news into a few sentences, and it's a skill that serves them well.

Saying what you are going to say

Practise an unprepared presentation in the following manner:

First, tell us what you are going to say in the next sentence, for example:

What are you going to say next?

"I am going to tell you about the awful trouble we're having—you know, it's in our team, all the extra demands that are being made on us—it's all because of the new unit—that's the financial guys—they keep on throwing stuff at us."

Then formulate a clear sentence in your mind and speak it out loud:

"We're having considerable difficulties in our team with all the extra demands coming from the new financial unit."

Then go on to the next idea:

What are you going to say then?

"Then I'm going to tell you about ..." and give your first version of the next idea, followed by the formulation of a single clear sentence ... and so on.

It helps if you have someone to listen to you and lead you through the exercise. Alternatively, record yourself.

Avoid the short hiatus between breath and speech

This might sound like a tautology when you are talking about stuttering and stammering, but many people who stutter have situations where they manage to avoid the hiatus (singing in rhythm for example) and other situations where the hiatus is exaggerated. Going from sensation and feeling straight into words avoids the hiatus, whereas thinking can create it, so practise feeling and expressing. You may find the 'scented breath' exercise in Chapter 11 helpful here.

Maintain your inner energy and enthusiasm

Your inner confidence makes an enormous difference to your voice, so keep your energy high and believe in yourself. If passion itself were to speak, how articulate it would be! The energy to speak comes from the whole of you, body as well as head. Let the body do the talking. The heart talks, the gut talks, the head often just gets in the way.

Help for stuttering

Psychologists have made exciting breakthroughs in helping people to overcome a stutter. If stuttering is a problem for you, you might like to consult Bobby Bodenhamer's research. He has had excellent results with people who stutter, and shares the fruit of his practice in his book, *Mastering Blocking and Stuttering: A Cognitive Approach to Achieving Fluency* (Carmarthen: Crown House, 2004). He offers various other useful resources at http://www.masteringstuttering. com.

How can I avoid my voice sounding breathy?

Some people like the sound of a breathy voice, particularly if it is low, and call it "sexy" or "alluring". If the voice is strained as well as breathy, it is sometimes called "husky" and admired for that. But anyone who can produce only a breathy or husky voice knows that it is tiring to produce and severely limits communication. Such a voice is incapable of light and shade, loudness and softness, which seriously limits a full range of communication. A habitual breathy or husky voice is usually a sign of damage to the vocal apparatus.

A breathy voice is caused by the vocal cords failing to come together adequately, so that air escapes. Of course, we can choose to speak in this way to create a particular effect. But if it is the *only* way you can speak, you may need to learn a different way of producing the voice by consulting a voice therapist or accessing medical help. The effect is most often due to damage to the vocal cords, such as swelling, nodules or cysts. In such cases you certainly need professional help.

How can I look after my voice?

The School of Health and Rehabilitation Sciences at Pittsburgh University estimates that at any one time between three and nine per cent of the population has some type of voice problem, from hoarseness or throat clearing and coughing to simple vocal fatigue and voice loss. Voice problems are the most common communication disorder.

Problems are most often due to the way a person uses her voice, an uncongenial physical environment or mental tension and stress. Usually a combination of these factors is present when a problem arises. Each factor taken separately is not particularly difficult to eliminate, and not particularly serious.

What are the first signs of trouble? Be aware early of any of the following and rest your voice if possible as soon as you notice one of them:

* tiredness or a feeling that talking is an effort
* a feeling of dryness in the throat or a tickling sensation
* a hot feeling or an ache in the throat
* a lump in the throat
* shortness of breath
* noisy breathing.

Before you even get to this stage, there are steps you can take to avoid problems. Let's start with the use of your voice.

Learn how to speak well!

As you are doing by reading this book! Adopt a comfortable, open posture. Relax your body, especially in the neck, shoulders and jaw. Breathe well. Speak at the pitch that is comfortable for you.

Give your voice a break

Any part of your body will get tired if you thrash it to death. So give your voice a break. When you consider that the average school teacher's vocal cords vibrate a couple of million times a day, it is clear that we have come to expect a lot from our voice. If you feel that your throat is dry and tired, or your voice is becoming hoarse, stop talking if you possibly can.

Avoid occasions where you have to speak for long periods without pause. Even a pause of a few seconds can make a difference.

Vary your voice. Give it lots of light and shade, so that you are not using your vocal cords at the same pitch and volume again and again. Have a quiet telephone-free day every now and then.

Don't abuse your voice – well not often anyway!

Your voice is not indestructible. In everyday communication, try not to overdo yelling, screaming, cheering or raucous singing. If you indulge, give your voice a good rest the day after!

Try not to shout above significant background noise. Don't carry out important conversations in noisy places, or if you feel you have to, use your mouth and lips and tongue to articulate well. At least people can then lip-read! Use a microphone if you have to speak in an over-large space or an environment with poor acoustics or competing noise.

To reduce or minimise voice misuse, use non-vocal or visual cues to attract attention, especially with a lively crowd such as group of children. Try not to speak at an unnatural pitch which can cause hoarseness.

If you strain and abuse your voice, you can damage the vocal chords. It's not worth it.

Stay healthy!

Your vocal cords are part of you and mirror your general well-being. If you are tired and rundown, your voice will reflect that, and will be particularly vulnerable at such times if you force it to perform beyond its capability. So, get sufficient rest, good food and exercise.

Rest your voice if you are unwell

When the vocal cords are inflamed or irritated due to infection, your voice is at its most vulnerable. You are more likely to upset the delicate balance of energies used to produce your voice when one part is not working well, and at such times it is easy to injure your vocal cords. If at all possible, give your voice a rest and time to recuperate from coughs, colds and sore throats before you use it to any great extent. A silent day at home when you have an infection which affects your voice could well save a week off work later on.

Take a steam inhalation

Your voice, nose and chest respond well to steam. It helps reduce swelling and irritation. The traditional way is to breathe in steam with a towel over your head over a bowl of steaming water but a hot steaming bath works well too.

Avoid clearing your throat too often

Excessive clearing of your throat is itself a sign that all is not well with your voice and that longer term you need to do some work on your vocal production. It can also be a sign of a medical condition. The act of clearing your throat is like hitting your vocal cords together and can make your voice even hoarser. You can get rid of excessive mucous by talking gently through it till your voice clears. Or drink a little water.

Avoid dehydrating drinks

The thin mucus that lubricates your vocal folds needs plenty of moisture. This is why it is best not to overindulge in substances that cause dehydration, such as alcohol, caffeinated coffee, tea and cola.

Warm your voice up

It is well worth warming up your voice before extensive use, just as a sportsman would warm up other parts of his body before working it hard.

Quit smoking

Smoking is clearly not a good idea either. Smoke breathed in causes irritation and swelling of the vocal cords. This eventually changes voice quality and flexibility permanently.

Avoid noxious atmospheres

Where possible avoid dry dusty conditions, smoke-filled rooms, chemical irritants and traffic fumes. Avoid becoming dehydrated, as speaking then irritates the vocal cords. Get a humidifier for your workplace.

Go to the doctor

Be aware that a sore throat or a weak debilitated voice could be symptoms of a medical problem, so consult a doctor if you are uncertain.

Having said all the above, your voice is a pretty robust instrument, and enjoys a good work out, so you don't need to treat it with kid gloves. Enjoy your voice and use it well.

You can find useful information on voice care at the Voice Care Network website: http://www.voicecare.org.uk

Where can I find a voice coach?

Voice coaching includes a broad spectrum of activities, from singing teaching to speech training and therapeutic voice work, and practitioners come with a variety of qualifications and skills. If you want voice help from an expert, be aware that there are various disciplines that cover voice and professionals will have trained in different ways. So know what you are getting!

The actor

A voice coach may well have an actor's training and a good coach with this background will have many skills to develop your ability to produce your voice well and create an impact with an audience. If you want an influential voice, make sure that you are also learning how to be authentic and connect strongly with people, not just how to project your voice and articulate clearly.

The singer

Alternatively, a voice coach may have a singing background. A good singer will be skilful in voice control, know healthy ways to expand the use of your voice and have good techniques for caring for your voice. Make sure that they understand the spoken voice as well as the singing voice, as special techniques are used to amplify the voice for public singing performance that don't apply to the spoken voice.

The NLP coach

As your voice is intimately connected to your psyche and sense of self you may well find that a rapid and effective way to remove vocal blocks will be to consult someone with in-depth experience of neurolinguistic programming. An NLP coach in a very few sessions (even a single session) can help you identify and work through the psychological or root causes of vocal difficulties.

If you can, find someone with voice experience as well as practical expertise in NLP. In the UK, a good place to start is the Association of NLP: http://www.anlp.org. There you will find good information and advice on NLP plus a list of practitioners.

The voice therapist

A voice therapist will help you correct potential damage to your voice and teach you how to produce your voice more effectively. A voice therapist does not usually help you to communicate with more impact.

It is a good idea to find someone who comes recommended and to experience one session to see if there is a good fit before signing up to a series of sessions.

You can find a list of voice therapists in the UK at http://www.singing-teachers.co.uk

You can also find some excellent speaking-voice coaches on the Natural Voice website which is mainly aimed at singers: http://www.naturalvoice.net/index.asp

See also the Voice and Speech Trainers Association at http://www.vasta.org

Where can I get assistance for serious voice problems?

If you have serious voice problems—if you have damaged your voice for example—you will need medical or therapeutic help. Try one of the following for further information:

The doctor

For most voice problems, your doctor will be your first point of call. Any hoarseness, breathiness, voice fading or pain that persists after a week or so should be reported to your doctor and investigated.

The consultant

Many times a voice problem is a symptom of a wider health problem which the doctor can address. Your doctor can arrange blood tests, X-rays and so on, and can refer you to an ear, nose and throat specialist or to a voice clinic to have your vocal cords checked out.

The voice clinic

Voice clinics, available in some areas, have a team that includes an ear, nose and throat surgeon, a speech therapist, and possibly an osteopath, physiotherapist and even a singing advisor and a psychologist.

Often a biopsy is carried out to examine the vocal cords and then surgery can remove damaged vocal tissue if necessary. I would consider surgery a last resort.

The British Voice Association has a list of voice clinics in the UK: http://www.british-voice-association.com/voice_clinics.htm

They also have an interesting collection of articles on voice: http://www.british-voice-association.com/archive.htm

Speech therapists

If the voice problem relates to the way you use your voice you can seek help from a speech therapist. The Association of Speech and Language Therapists in Independent Practice has a list of therapists grouped under areas in the UK: http://www.helpwithtalking.com

All ASLTIP therapists are certified members of the Royal College of Speech and Language Therapists (MRCSLT) and are registered with the Health Professions Council.

The singing advisor, physiotherapist, osteopath

You can also get advice on the way you use your voice from a singing advisor. You may also find the expertise of a physiotherapist or osteopath helpful.

The Voice Foundation website has a useful section on how to tackle voice problems as well as other voice information: http://www.voicefoundation.org

Good luck with your voice journey!

Notes

1. Malcolm Gladwell, *Blink: The Power of Thinking without Thinking* (London: Allen Lane, 2005).

2. *SGI Quarterly*, July 2004.

3. Fritz Perls, *Gestalt Therapy Verbatim* (Lafyette, CA: Real People Press, 1969), 57.

4. Male and female pronouns and adjectives are used indiscriminately through the book.

5. Alexander Lowen, *Bioenergetics* (New York: Coward, McCann & Geoghegan, Inc., 1975).

6. Bobby G. Bodenhamer, *Mastering Blocking and Stuttering: A Cognitive Approach to Achieving Fluency* (Carmarthen: Crown House, 2004).

7. Jerzy Grotowski, *Towards a Poor Theatre* (New York: Simon & Schuster, 1968).

8. *Blackadder Goes Forth*, BBC TV series, 1989.

9. Compiled and first used by the London Shakespeare Workout's Prison Project in 1998. Available at http://www.londonshakespeare.org.uk/prison/

10. Interview with Andy Tongue in the *Olympic Review*. Available at http://www.olympic.org/upload/news/olympic_review/review_20071259368_UK.pdf

11. Stephen Denning, *The Leader's Guide to Storytelling: Mastering the Art and Discipline of Business Narrative* (San Francisco, CA: Jossey-Bass, 2005).

12 G. W. E. Russell, *Collections and Recollections* (New York: Harper, 1898).

13. Tim Gallwey, *The Inner Game of Tennis* (New York: Random House, 1974).

14. Kristin Linklater, *Freeing the Natural Voice* (Drama Publishers, 1976). 2nd edition Nick Hern Books London 2006.

15. *Liar Liar*, directed by Tom Shadyack, 1997.

16. Malidoma Patrice Somé, *Of Water and the Spirit* (New York: Tarcher/ Putnam, 1994).

17. Rachel Remen, *My Grandfather's Blessings* (New York: Riverhead Books, 2000).

18. A phrase first coined by Angela R. Garber in "Death By Powerpoint" in April 2001. Available at http://www.smallbusinesscomputing. com/biztools/article.php/684871

19. Hal Milton, *Going Public: A Practical Guide to Developing Personal Charisma* (Deerfield Beach, FL: HCI, 1995).

20. Carlos Castaneda, *The Art of Dreaming* (New York: HarperCollins, 1993).

21. Recounted in Mihaly Csikszentmihalyi, *Flow: The Psychology of Optimal Experience* (New York: Harper and Row, 1996).

22. Lleyton Hewitt in a BBC interview, 5 July 2002.

23. Tim Gallwey, *The Inner Game of Tennis* (New York: Random House, 1974).

24. Gabrielle Roth, *Maps to Ecstacy, A Healing Journey for the Untamed Spirit* (Novato, CA: New World Library, 1989).

25. Agnes de Mille, *Martha: The Life and Work of Martha Graham* (New York: Random House, 1991).

Index

Praise for *Voice of Influence*

A thoroughly enjoyable and engaging read that mixes practical advice and easy to follow exercises with deep insight. In this book Judy conveys how our voice is a gift to be treasured and celebrated.

Alan Briscoe
Positive Choices Project Manager, Mind Cymru

For those of you who don't have the money to use a voice coach then this is the best place to start. Your voice is your "Blueprint" and reveals so much about ourselves, so why not show others who you are at your best? This is a very practical book, giving sound advice and easy hints, tips and exercises that will help most people build their impact and influence. Thank you, Judy, for sharing your knowledge and experiences.

Caroline Harding
Director of Learning & Development, Herbert Smith LLP

Learning is always fun with Judy. This book is thoroughly readable, insightful and original. It achieves its serious learning objectives in an imaginative, inspiring and enjoyable way. Judy's enthusiasm and knowledge of her subject shine through every page. This book should be on the reading list of anyone who wants to learn how to communicate more effectively and how to be more authentic and charismatic in putting across their messages.

Celia Morris
Training & Development Manager, Railways,
Mott MacDonald Ltd

This book is very timely, and attuned to an expanding awareness of the importance of voice as a key factor in effective leadership and management. Increasing attention is also being paid to the effects of sound on people at work, at leisure and at home.

It's widely acknowledged that different beats and rhythms can have dramatic effects on both mood and productivity; and we are rebelling against dulling, dreadful "muzak" in our public places by retreating into a personal "iPod" world. We know that babies and children respond differently to soothing as opposed to strident sounds, but have we really given thought to how and if our own voices truly express the essence of ourselves and thereby affect the way we are perceived at work and in our personal lives?

Judy Apps's new book, *Voice of Influence*, explores these issues, and many more. I know from experience that Judy's methods and concepts are highly effective and relevant in a world where the competition for "air time" means it is increasingly difficult to garner the attention we need to get our authentic message across clearly and congruently. I am certain that many coaches, managers and senior executives—and parents too—will benefit from learning how to use the voice as a tool for improving communications and responsiveness.

Christine Miller
Author and Founder Editor, *ReSource Magazine*

This book will strike a chord with even the most experienced speaker—everyone can improve. My work with Judy has been invaluable—enjoy the read.

David Maloney
Business Development Director

Judy Apps is a great communicator and teacher. In this book she brings the subject to life with exercises and anecdotes that inspire and challenge. Her easy style makes makes the book absorbing and fun. I would recommend it for anyone who wants to get more from life through more authentic communication.

Jackie Potter
Chief Executive Officer, Corridor Manchester

Voice of Influence by Judy Apps is an exploration of voice and being. It includes plenty of technical processes to improve and use our voice, connecting it more deeply to our inner and outer worlds. A must for the professional speaker from business person to actor.

Judith Delozier
Delozier and Associates International

This accessible guide by voice coach and NLP trainer Judy Apps, is a fascinating mind–body approach to finding your authentic voice and expressing yourself with integrity, presence and passion.

Grounded in straightforward technical expertise, packed with activities and tips, it offers insight and practical advice on transforming limiting beliefs and emotional blocks to change forever your public speaking, your training, coaching and even your personal conversations.

Highly recommended for anyone wanting to be more confident, inspiring, effective and more fully themselves in their communication.

Judith Lowe
NLP Trainer, PPD Learning Ltd

Reading this book was a sheer delight. Judy's book offers us a profound and compelling message about how our voice links our inner and outer worlds. This message is set out with such a light touch as we are invited into a world of breath, of voice, of emotion and intention alongside excellent technical information, tips and how-to's—an irresistible combination.

As someone who has been aware of the sound of my own and others voices for many years, I come from a family who love to sing, I am aware that the sound and the "feel" of one's voice can be both revealing and engaging. Breath and voice connect what is happening in our inner world, consciously and unconsciously, with how we are in the external public part of our life. Judy tells us why this is so and opens up the possibility to be active and intentional in engaging with our voice, improving and changing our voice, while at the same time remaining true to who we are in the world.

Mary Mc Phail
Chief Executive, World Association of Girl Guides and
Girl Scouts

Judy Apps provides a generous range of insights about breath, the body and the voice which are essential yet often neglected aspects of the art of communication.

Full of practical tips, this book demonstrates how you can enhance your ability to speak confidently and authentically in a public setting—whether one-to-one or in front of a large audience.

In her clear and friendly style, Judy uses practical exercises and stories to explain how to develop greater control over your voice. By focusing on your breathing, and your whole body state, the kind of sounds you make will express who you are more authentically, so that other people will not only listen to you, but take notice of what you have to say.

The voice is far more than a "neutral" conveyer of messages. As you attune your ears to how someone's voice sounds, you'll be picking up far more information about them: their internal state, their attitude, the degree to which they are present, and so on—factors which influence the meaning you make of their communication.

Peter Young
Author of *Understanding NLP*

I can already see the significant benefits if someone wants a guide on how best to prepare physically and psychologically for public speaking, presentations or promotions. It brought back to me so many useful, practical and straightforward tips to adopt and helps you to really understand what a marvellous piece of kit the body is. Judy, your book highlights the subtle ways that each of us can put into everyday use to articulate clearly how we feel and how we want others to react to us. Each of our voices cannot be ignored. We all have a right to be heard, so it is incumbent on all of us to make the most of it, whatever we do and whenever we need it.

Richard Owen
Chief Executive Officer, Real Estate & Construction

About the author

Judy Apps

A voice coach, qualified at the Royal College of Music, London and the Conservatorio S. Cecilia in Rome, and a member of the International Coaching Federation and the University Global.

Combining the skills of a performing arts and business management background, Judy has many years of experience in coaching and in developing creative training programmes. Her innovative techniques, combined with an incisive, encouraging approach, have enabled many executives to achieve great leaps in their ability to communicate and lead, and in their sense of personal confidence.

A member of the International Coaching Federation and the NLP University Global Trainers' and Consultants' Network, she has had notable success coaching top executives in many corporations and organisations.

Voice of Influence workshops

She runs regular Voice of Influence workshops in London and elsewhere. For more information visit: http://www.voiceofinfluence.co.uk

or you can contact Judy personally at judy@voiceofinfluence.co.uk